Into The Wild

Poetry from The

Animal Kingdom

Titles also, by Dave Charles

The Consequences of War – Contemporary Poetry, and Haiku about War, Conflict, and PTSD.

The Scottish Wilderness – Poetry, and Haiku about Scotland, Nature, Places, Lochs, and Glens.

The Jilted Generation – Poetry, Haiku, and Narrative Poetry about Emotions, Life Stories, and Nature.

Ancient Astronaut Theorists Compendium of Poetry and Short Stories – The Ancient Alien Agenda, Reports of Sightings, Ancient Locations on Earth, and Out-of-Place Artefacts Found on our Planet.

Finding Inner Peace - PTSD Survivors Guide, Poetry, and Helpful Information to Find Inner Peace, and to Aid Recovery.

Between Heaven and Earth – A Guide to Majestic Scottish Castles, Best Castle Gardens, Monuments, Tourist Attractions, Battle Sites, Golf Courses, Beaches, and Whisky Distilleries.

Treasure Hunting the Ultimate Guide – All Aspects of Metal Detecting, Gold Panning, Relic, Fossil and Gemstone Hunting, Magnet Fishing, Bottle Digging, River Hunting, Shipwreck Diving and Much More.

Into The Wild

Anthology of Wildlife
Poetry, Haiku,
and Short Stories
from
The Animal Kingdom

Dave Charles

For my Children

I know how much they love animals

About the Author

I was born in Oxford, England, then moved to Manchester aged six. I left school at sixteen and joined the British Army, where I spent two years at an army college, before starting my adult service.

This anthology of poems is a mixture of rhyming, haiku, and narrative short stories from the animal kingdom.

I served in the British Army for many years. I am a veteran of the late Cold War era, having served in the former West Germany between 1984 and 1989.

I later served in Saudi Arabia and Iraq during the first Persian Gulf War in 1991 as part of 'Operation Granby' or as the U.S. termed 'Desert Storm'. I then served with the United Nations, undertaking peacekeeping tours in Cyprus and Bosnia during the 1990's. I also served in many other countries, including twice in Canada.

After leaving the armed forces, I was diagnosed with complex combat PTSD and numerous other medical conditions.

Writing poetry and short stories has been a kind of therapy for me and a huge part of my recovery process.

The Beauty of Wildlife

The beauty of wildlife is a source of inspiration for poets and nature lovers alike. From the majestic lion to the delicate butterfly, each creature in the animal kingdom holds a unique allure that captivates our hearts and minds. In the world of wildlife poetry, these creatures are celebrated through verse, capturing the essence of their beauty and grace in words that resonate with readers.

In the vast expanse of the natural world, there is a poetry that speaks to the soul. The symphony of the forest, the dance of the ocean, and the whispers of the wind all inspire poets to pen verses that pay tribute to the beauty of wildlife. Through their words, poets transport us to a realm where we can witness the wonders of nature in all its glory, from the soaring eagle to the gentle deer.

Wildlife poetry is a celebration of the diversity and splendour of the animal kingdom. Each poem is a tribute to the unique qualities of a particular species, highlighting its characteristics and behaviours in a way that evokes a sense of wonder and admiration. Whether it is a poem about the strength of the elephant or the grace of the swan, wildlife poetry allows us to connect with the natural world on a deeper level, fostering a sense of appreciation and respect for all living creatures.

Through the power of language, poets convey the magic of nature in all its forms, inviting readers to embark on a journey of exploration and discovery. From the roar of the lion to the flutter of the butterfly's wings, each poem in this collection is a testament to the awe-inspiring beauty of wildlife.

So let us immerse ourselves in the world of wildlife poetry and revel in the beauty of the natural world. Let us savour the words that paint vivid portraits of creatures both great and small, and let us be inspired by the wonders of nature that surround us.

This anthology of poetry is a combination of traditional rhyming poetry, haiku and narrative stories about wildlife and creatures from the animal kingdom. I hope you enjoy them.

The Importance of Wildlife Sanctuaries

Wildlife sanctuaries play a crucial role in preserving the natural habitats of various species of animals and plants. These sanctuaries provide a safe haven for wildlife to thrive and flourish without the threat of human interference or exploitation. They serve as important breeding grounds and help in maintaining the delicate balance of ecosystems. By protecting these sanctuaries, we are ensuring the survival of countless species for future generations to enjoy and appreciate.

In addition to their ecological importance, wildlife sanctuaries also hold significant cultural and spiritual value. Many indigenous communities around the world have deep connections to the land and the animals that inhabit these sanctuaries. These places are often considered sacred and are integral to the cultural identity of these communities. By preserving wildlife sanctuaries, we are also honouring and respecting the traditions and beliefs of these indigenous peoples.

From a poetic perspective, wildlife sanctuaries provide endless inspiration for poets and writers. The beauty and diversity of the natural world found within these sanctuaries offer a rich tapestry of imagery and symbolism to draw upon in creating evocative and moving poems. The sights, sounds, and smells of these sanctuaries can transport readers to another world, where they can experience the wonder and awe of the natural world through the power of poetry.

For poetry lovers, exploring the themes of conservation, preservation, and the interconnectedness of all living beings through the lens of wildlife sanctuaries can be a deeply enriching and fulfilling experience. Poems celebrating the beauty and resilience of wildlife found within these sanctuaries can serve as a powerful reminder of the importance of protecting and preserving these precious habitats for future generations. Through poetry, we can raise awareness and inspire others to act in safeguarding these sanctuaries for the benefit of all life on Earth.

In conclusion, the importance of wildlife sanctuaries cannot be overstated. They are vital to the survival of countless species, hold cultural and spiritual significance, and provide endless inspiration for poets and writers. By recognising and honouring the value of these sanctuaries, we are not only preserving the natural world but also enriching our own lives through the beauty and wonder of the wildlife that inhabit them. Let us continue to celebrate and protect these sanctuaries through the power of poetry and ensure a brighter future for all living beings.

The Majestic Lion

In the vast plains of Africa, the majestic lion reigns supreme as the king of beasts. With its golden mane flowing in the wind and piercing eyes that exude power and strength, the lion is a symbol of courage and majesty in the animal kingdom. The lion's roar can be heard from miles away, a powerful sound that strikes fear into the hearts of its prey and commands respect from all who hear it. Its mighty paws and razor-sharp teeth make it a formidable predator, capable of taking down even the largest of animals with ease.

But despite its fearsome reputation, the lion is also a social creature, forming strong bonds with its pride members and caring for its young with tenderness and love. Watching a lioness playfully nuzzle her cubs or a pride lounging in the sun together is a sight that warms the hearts of even the most hardened of souls.

For animal lovers, the lion represents the beauty and power of the natural world, a reminder of the importance of protecting and preserving our planet's wildlife. Through poetry and art, we can celebrate the majesty of the lion and all creatures that roam the earth, inspiring others to join us in our mission to protect and cherish these magnificent animals.

So let us raise our voices in praise of the majestic lion, a symbol of strength, courage, and beauty in the wild. May we always strive to protect and honour these magnificent creatures, ensuring that future generations can continue to marvel at their splendour for years to come.

The Graceful Deer

In the vast expanse of the wild, there roams a creature of grace and beauty - the deer. With its slender legs and gentle eyes, the deer embodies a sense of elegance that captivates all who encounter it in the forest.

The graceful deer moves through the trees with a lightness that seems to defy gravity. Its hooves barely make a sound as it navigates the undergrowth, its delicate ears perked up to catch the slightest rustle of leaves or snap of a twig.

The deer's keen senses are finely tuned to the rhythms of the natural world, allowing it to blend seamlessly into its surroundings and evade predators with ease.

For animal lovers and wildlife enthusiasts alike, the deer holds a special place in our hearts. Its peaceful presence in the forest reminds us of the delicate balance of nature and the importance of preserving the habitats of these magnificent creatures. Through poetry and art, we can celebrate the beauty of the deer and all the wonders of the natural world.

Whether you are a seasoned wildlife enthusiast or simply someone who appreciates the beauty of the natural world, the graceful deer will inspire you to see these creatures in a new light and deepen your appreciation for the wonders of the animal kingdom.

The Mysterious Wolf

In the heart of the dense forest, there lived a mysterious wolf, known only by whispers and howls in the night. Its coat was a deep, shadowy black, blending seamlessly with the shadows of the trees. Its eyes were like orbs of amber fire, glowing with an otherworldly light.

Animal lovers and wildlife enthusiasts would often catch glimpses of the wolf, fleeting and elusive, disappearing into the mist before they could get a closer look. Some said it was the spirit of the forest, a guardian watching over the creatures that called the wilderness home.

The mysterious wolf inspired awe and fear in equal measure. Its presence was a reminder of the untamed beauty and power of the natural world, a symbol of the wild heart that beat in all living creatures.

Poets and storytellers spun tales of the mysterious wolf, weaving its legend into the fabric of the forest. They wrote of its silent grace, its haunting howls that echoed through the trees, and the way it moved like a wraith through the undergrowth.

For animal lovers and the general public alike, the mysterious wolf held a special place in their hearts. It was a symbol of the unknown, a creature of mystery and magic that captivated the imagination.

The Soaring Eagle

In the vast expanse of the sky, the eagle reigns supreme. With wings outstretched, it soars effortlessly, a symbol of strength and freedom. The magnificent bird of prey commands the attention of all who witness its graceful flight.

The eagle holds a special place in our hearts. Its keen eyesight and powerful talons remind us of the raw beauty and power of nature. Watching an eagle in flight is a truly awe-inspiring experience, a reminder of the untamed wilderness that still exists in our world.

In the world of animal poetry, the eagle is a frequent muse. Poets have long been captivated by its majesty, using its image as a metaphor for courage, wisdom, and the indomitable spirit of the wild. The soaring eagle embodies the essence of freedom, a reminder that we are all connected to the natural world in ways we may not always understand.

As we gaze upon the soaring eagle, let us be reminded of the importance of preserving our natural habitats and protecting the creatures that call them home. Let us be inspired by the grace and power of this magnificent bird and strive to live our lives with the same sense of purpose and freedom.

So, the next time you find yourself in the presence of an eagle, take a moment to appreciate its beauty and strength. Let its soaring flight remind you of the wild heart that beats within us all, and the untamed beauty of the natural world that surrounds us.

The Melodic Nightingale

In the stillness of the night, a sweet and melodious sound fills the air. It is the song of the nightingale, a small bird with a powerful voice that captivates all who listen. Its beautiful melody echoes through the trees, bringing a sense of peace and tranquillity to the surrounding wilderness.

For animal lovers, the nightingale holds a special place in their hearts. Its delicate appearance and enchanting song make it a favourite among bird enthusiasts. The nightingale's voice is said to be one of the most beautiful in the animal kingdom, capable of expressing a wide range of emotions from joy to sorrow.

The nightingale represents the beauty and mystery of the natural world, reminding us of the wonders that exist beyond our own human experience.

As wildlife enthusiasts, we are drawn to the nightingale's ability to thrive in the wild, despite the challenges it faces. Its resilience and determination serve as a reminder of the strength and adaptability of all living creatures.

So let us take a moment to appreciate the melodic nightingale, a symbol of beauty and grace in the animal kingdom. May its song continue to inspire us and remind us of the magic that exists in the world.

The Playful Hummingbird

In the bustling world of the animal kingdom, there is one creature that stands out for its unique charm and energy - the playful hummingbird. With its iridescent feathers and rapid wing beats, this tiny bird captivates all who have the privilege of witnessing its aerial acrobatics.

The hummingbird is a symbol of joy and freedom, darting from flower to flower with a seemingly boundless energy. Its delicate frame belies a fierce determination to survive and thrive in even the most challenging of environments. To watch a hummingbird in action is to witness nature's poetry in motion.

As animal lovers and wildlife enthusiasts, we are drawn to the hummingbird not only for its beauty but also for its resilience. Despite its small size, the hummingbird is a mighty force in the ecosystem, pollinating flowers and contributing to the biodiversity of its habitat.

So let us raise a toast to the playful hummingbird, a symbol of joy and beauty in the wild. May we always remember to cherish and protect these tiny wonders of nature, for they bring a touch of magic to our world and remind us of the importance of preserving the delicate balance of life on Earth.

The Powerful Orca

In the vast ocean, there is a creature like no other - the powerful Orca. Also known as the killer whale, this majestic animal commands respect and awe with its sleek black and white body, and intelligent eyes that seem to hold the secrets of the deep.

The Orca is a symbol of strength and grace, a predator at the top of the food chain. With its sharp teeth and powerful tail, it hunts for seals, fish, and sometimes even other whales. But despite its fearsome reputation, the Orca is also a highly social and intelligent animal, known to travel in pods and communicate through a complex system of clicks and whistles.

For animal lovers, the Orca represents the beauty and mystery of the ocean. Its playful nature and acrobatic displays have captivated audiences around the world, inspiring awe and wonder in those who have had the privilege of witnessing these magnificent creatures in their natural habitat.

The Orca is a creature that commands attention and respect. Its presence in the ocean is a reminder of the delicate balance of nature, and the importance of protecting these magnificent animals for future generations to enjoy.

The Colourful Clownfish

In the vibrant world beneath the waves,
Where coral reefs shimmer and sway,
The clownfish dances with grace,
Its colours brightening up the ocean's maze.

With hues of orange, white, and black,
This tiny fish stands out in a pack,
Its playful nature bringing joy,
To all who watch this underwater ploy.

Living in symbiosis with the sea anemone,
The clownfish finds safety and harmony,
In the swaying tentacles of its host,
A unique relationship that should be boasted.

With its curious eyes and cheerful demeanour,
The clownfish is a true ocean dreamer,
Swimming through the waters with ease,
A sight that always seems to please.

So let us marvel at this colourful creature,
And treasure its presence as a special feature,
Of the vast and wondrous marine world,
Where every fish, big or small, is unfurled.

For in the depths of the ocean blue,
The clownfish shines in a brilliant hue,
A reminder of the beauty that lies below,
And the magic of the underwater show.

So let us protect this precious treasure,
And ensure that it thrives beyond measure,
For the clownfish and all its kin,
Deserve a world where they can swim and grin.

The Gentle Sea Turtle

The gentle sea turtle glides through the ocean with grace and beauty, captivating the hearts of all who are lucky enough to witness its elegant movements. In the vast expanse of the sea, the sea turtle is a symbol of resilience and wisdom, embodying the mysteries of the deep blue.

With its large, flippers propelling it forward, the sea turtle navigates the waters with ease, a true master of its environment. Its shell, a protective armour that has evolved over millions of years, is a testament to the strength and endurance of this remarkable creature.

For animal lovers, general public, and wildlife enthusiasts alike, the sea turtle serves as a reminder of the importance of conservation and respect for all living beings. Its presence in the pages of this book is a call to action, urging readers to protect and preserve the delicate ecosystems that are home to these incredible animals.

In the realm of animal poetry and wildlife poetry, the gentle sea turtle stands out as a symbol of hope and inspiration. Its peaceful demeanour and quiet strength remind us of the interconnectedness of all living beings, and the importance of living in harmony with the natural world.

The Wise Owl

In the dark of night, when all is still,
The Wise Owl perches upon his hill.
With eyes that gleam like golden light,
He watches over the world with all his might.

His feathers soft, his talons strong,
The Wise Owl knows where he belongs.
In the forest deep, or the meadow wide,
He soars through the air with effortless glide.

With wisdom beyond his years,
The Wise Owl silences all fears.
He speaks not a word, but his presence alone,
Fills the night with a sense of calm unknown.

To those who listen, he imparts his lore,
Teaching lessons of life and so much more.
For the Wise Owl sees through the veil of night,
Guiding us towards the path that's right.

So if you ever feel lost or alone,
Look to the sky, where the Wise Owl is flown.
For in his eyes, you'll find the truth,
And in his wings, the wisdom of youth.

May we all learn from the Wise Owl's gaze,
And cherish the lessons of his days.
For in the silence of the night,
He teaches us to live with insight.

The Curious Squirrel

In the heart of the forest, where the sunlight filters through the canopy of trees, there lives a curious squirrel named Willow. With her bushy tail and bright eyes, she scampers through the branches, always on the lookout for new adventures.

Willow is a creature of boundless curiosity, always eager to explore the world around her. She is fascinated by the birds that sing in the treetops, the insects that buzz in the undergrowth, and the gentle rustling of the leaves in the wind. Every day brings a new discovery for Willow, a new mystery to unravel.

But Willow's favourite pastime is watching the humans who pass through the forest. She perches on a branch high above the ground, hidden from view, and observes their comings and goings with keen interest. She marvels at their strange ways, their loud voices, and their clumsy movements. To Willow, they are like creatures from another world, a world she can only glimpse from afar.

As the seasons change and the days grow shorter, Willow's curiosity only deepens. She watches as the leaves turn from green to gold, as the animals prepare for the long winter ahead, and as the forest settles into a peaceful slumber. And through it all, she remains ever curious, ever eager to learn more about the world she calls home.

For those who love animals, who feel a kinship with the creatures of the wild, Willow's story is a reminder of the wonder and beauty that surrounds us every day. In her boundless curiosity, in her thirst for knowledge, she embodies the spirit of the forest itself – untamed, wild, and utterly captivating.

The Elusive Fox

In the depths of the forest, hidden from sight,
Lives a creature of cunning, swift and bright.
The elusive fox, with its fiery red coat,
Moves like a shadow, silent and remote.

For those who seek to catch a glimpse,
Must be patient, quiet, and willing to wince.
For the fox is a master of disguise,
Blending seamlessly with earth and skies.

Its eyes, like amber jewels, gleam in the night,
Watching, waiting, ready to take flight.
A symbol of wisdom, sly and clever,
The fox has stories it will never sever.

To see a fox is a rare delight,
A fleeting moment, a magical sight.
For those who love the wild and free,
The fox is a creature to admire and see.

So let us cherish this elusive friend,
For its beauty and grace will never end.
In the heart of the forest, where shadows play,
The fox will dance and roam, forever and a day.

For animal lovers and wildlife enthusiasts alike,
The fox is a symbol of nature's might.
In poems and stories, its legend will endure,
A creature of mystery, wild and pure.

The Plight of the Rhinoceros

In the heart of the African savannah, a majestic creature roams with grace and power - the rhinoceros. But behind its strong exterior lies a heartbreaking truth - the rhinoceros is facing a silent war, a battle for survival that threatens to wipe out this iconic species from the face of the earth.

Poachers, driven by greed and ignorance, hunt the rhinoceros for its prized horn, believed to have medicinal properties in some cultures. As a result, the rhinoceros' population has plummeted to dangerously low levels, pushing these magnificent creatures to the brink of extinction.

But there is hope. Conservationists and wildlife enthusiasts are rallying together to protect the rhinoceros and preserve its natural habitat. Through education, awareness, and anti-poaching efforts, we can make a difference and ensure a future for these gentle giants.

As animal lovers, it is our duty to speak up for those who cannot speak for themselves. The rhinoceros needs our help now more than ever. We must stand together, raise our voices, and take action to save this incredible species from disappearing forever.

Let us celebrate the beauty and resilience of the rhinoceros through poetry and art. Let us honour its strength and spirit, and pledge to protect it for generations to come. Together, we can make a difference and ensure that the plight of the rhinoceros does not end in tragedy, but in triumph.

The Endangered Pangolin

The pangolin, a unique and fascinating creature, is sadly one of the most endangered animals on the planet. Known for its distinctive scaly armour and long, sticky tongue, the pangolin is often referred to as the "scaly anteater" due to its diet of ants and termites. However, despite its remarkable features, the pangolin is facing a grave threat to its survival.

Illegal poaching and trafficking of pangolins for their meat and scales have driven these creatures to the brink of extinction. In some cultures, pangolin scales are believed to have medicinal properties, leading to a high demand for these animals in the illegal wildlife trade. As a result, all eight species of pangolins are now listed as either vulnerable, endangered, or critically endangered by the International Union for Conservation of Nature.

For animal lovers, general public, and wildlife enthusiasts alike, the endangered pangolin serves as a poignant reminder of the importance of conservation efforts in safeguarding our planet's precious wildlife. Let us come together to protect the pangolin and ensure that future generations can continue to marvel at these extraordinary animals in the wild.

The Struggle of the Giant Panda

In the lush bamboo forests of China,
A gentle giant roams free,
But the future of the panda is uncertain,
And its struggles we must see.

Once revered as a symbol of peace,
The panda now faces threats,
From habitat loss to poaching,
Its survival hangs by threads.

With black and white fur so iconic,
The panda captures our hearts,
But behind its cute exterior,
Lies a story of despair and smarts.

Endangered and vulnerable,
The panda fights to survive,
But with our help and protection,
It can continue to thrive.

Through conservation efforts and awareness,
We can ensure the panda's fate,
For this majestic creature deserves our love,
And a world where it can mate.

So let us come together,
Animal lovers, wildlife enthusiasts alike,
To protect the panda and its home,
And ensure its future is bright.

For in the struggle of the giant panda,
We find a reflection of our own,
A reminder of the fragility of life,
And the importance of a world where all creatures are
known.

So let us stand united,
In the fight for the panda's plight,
And together we can make a difference,
And ensure its future is bright.

The Call of the Forest

In the heart of the forest, where ancient trees whisper tales of old, there is a call that beckons to all who listen. It is the call of the forest, a song of nature that speaks to the soul of every creature that roams its leafy depths.

For animal lovers, life on earth is a symphony of sights and sounds that blend together in perfect harmony. From the playful antics of squirrels to the majestic beauty of deer, each creature plays its part in the grand performance of life in the forest.

For wildlife enthusiasts, the call of the forest is a siren song that lures them into its mysterious depths. They are captivated by the wild beauty of the creatures that call the forest home, and they find solace in the peaceful embrace of nature's embrace.

In the world of nature-inspired animal poetry, the call of the forest is a recurring theme that evokes a sense of wonder and awe. Poets weave tales of wolves howling at the moon, of owls hooting in the night, and of bears lumbering through the undergrowth. Each poem is a love letter to the wild creatures that roam the forest, celebrating their beauty and resilience in the face of a changing world.

But not all poetry is serious in nature. Humorous animal poetry also finds a home in the forest, where mischievous raccoons play pranks on unsuspecting campers and wise old owls dispense cryptic advice to lost travellers. These poems bring a light-hearted touch to the world of wildlife, reminding us that even in the darkest of forests, there is room for laughter and joy.

The Mischievous Monkeys

In the heart of the jungle, where the trees reach high and the sun barely kisses the forest floor, dwell the mischievous monkeys. These playful creatures swing from branch to branch with ease, their chatter filling the air with excitement and energy.

Their antics are legendary among the other inhabitants of the jungle, from the graceful tigers to the wise old elephants. The monkeys are always up to something, whether it's stealing fruit from a nearby village or playing pranks on unsuspecting passersby.

But despite their mischievous ways, the monkeys are beloved by all who call the jungle home. Their laughter is infectious, and their acrobatic skills are truly a sight to behold. They remind us to never take life too seriously, and to always find joy in the simplest of moments.

The Playful Penguins

In the icy realms of the South Pole, where the snow meets the sea, there exists a charming and lively group of creatures known as the playful penguins. These endearing birds waddle and slide across the frozen landscape with grace and agility, their black and white feathers glistening in the sunlight.

With their comical antics and playful personalities, penguins never fail to bring a smile to the faces of those who watch them frolic in the frigid waters. Their synchronized swimming and synchronized waddling are a sight to behold, a true testament to the beauty and wonder of the natural world.

The Laughing Hyena

In the African savannah, there is a creature known for its distinctive laugh that echoes through the night – the hyena. With its cackling call that can be heard for miles, the hyena is a symbol of both fear and fascination in the wild.

With its sharp teeth and scavenging ways, the hyena may not be everyone's favourite animal, but there is no denying its place in the natural world. From its haunting cries to its comical antics, the hyena embodies the wild spirit of the African wilderness.

So come along on this journey through the savannah, where the hyena's laugh rings out like a melody in the night, reminding us of the magic and mystery of the natural world. Let us raise a toast to the laughing hyena, a true character of the wild.

The Angry Alligator

In the heart of the swamp, where the water is murky and the cypress trees loom tall, there lived an alligator unlike any other. This particular alligator was known far and wide as "The Angry Alligator," for his fierce temper and short fuse.

The Angry Alligator spent his days lurking in the shadows, waiting for unsuspecting prey to wander too close to his domain. With a thunderous roar and a snap from his jaws, he would strike, leaving chaos and fear in his wake. The other animals in the swamp knew how to steer clear of this dangerous creature, for his anger knew no bounds.

But deep down, beneath his tough exterior, The Angry Alligator was simply misunderstood. He had faced hardships and challenges in his life that had left him bitter and resentful. If only someone would take the time to see past his anger and show him kindness, perhaps he could learn to let go of his rage and find peace within himself.

One day, a brave little otter decided to approach The Angry Alligator, armed only with a kind heart and a gentle spirit. To everyone's surprise, the alligator did not lash out in anger. Instead, he listened as the otter spoke words of compassion and understanding. Slowly but surely, the walls around The Angry Alligator's heart began to crumble, and he allowed himself to trust and be vulnerable.

From that day on, The Angry Alligator was no more. In his place stood a creature filled with gratitude and love, ready to embrace the beauty of the natural world and all the creatures that called it home. And so, the swamp became a place of harmony and peace, all thanks to the power of compassion and forgiveness.

The Bouncing Kangaroo

In the vast Outback of Australia, where the sun beats down and the red earth stretches for miles, lives the bouncing kangaroo. With legs like springs and a tail for balance, this iconic marsupial is a sight to behold.

In the early morning light, the kangaroo emerges from its restful slumber, ready to start the day with a hop and a skip. With boundless energy and grace, it bounces across the rugged terrain, effortlessly leaping over obstacles in its path.

As the sun sets on the horizon, the kangaroo gathers with its fellow roos, creating a mesmerizing sight as they move in unison, a sea of bouncing bodies against the backdrop of the setting sun. Their movements are poetry in motion, a celebration of life on earth and the beauty of the natural world.

But don't be fooled by their playful antics – kangaroos are also fierce protectors of their young and will defend their territory with strength and determination. Their loyalty to their family unit is unwavering, a testament to the bonds that exist in the animal kingdom.

So let us raise a toast to the bouncing kangaroo, a symbol of resilience, agility, and the untamed spirit of the wild. May we always be inspired by their boundless energy and zest for life, reminding us to embrace our own inner strength and bounce through life with grace and determination.

The Polar Bear

In the far reaches of the Arctic, where the icy winds howl,
Lives a majestic creature, with fur as white as the snow
owl.
The polar bear, a symbol of strength and resilience,
Adapted to survive in the harshest of environments with
brilliance.

A master of the frozen tundra, with paws like snowshoes,
He roams the vast expanse, in search of seals to pursue.
With a keen sense of smell and sharp claws for hunting,
The polar bear is truly a force of nature, never shunning.

His coat of white camouflages him in the endless snow,
A ghostly figure, moving silently, with a graceful flow.
But beneath his imposing exterior lies a tender heart,
A mother fiercely protective of her cubs, never apart.

In a world threatened by climate change and melting ice,
The polar bear faces challenges, a tragic sacrifice.
We must strive to protect this magnificent beast,
Preserve his habitat, so his beauty will never cease.

So let us raise our voices in celebration and cheer,
For the polar bear, a symbol of the wild, so dear.
May his spirit inspire us to cherish and conserve,
The wonders of nature, for all creatures to preserve.

The Serene Streams

In the heart of the forest, where the trees whisper secrets to the wind, lies a place of unparalleled beauty - the serene streams. These gentle waterways meander through the landscape, weaving their way through the lush greenery and providing a haven for all manner of creatures.

For animal lovers, the streams are a treasure trove of wildlife. Ducks paddle lazily along the surface, their vibrant feathers shining in the sunlight. Fish dart beneath the clear waters, their silvery scales glinting as they navigate the rocky bottom. And on the banks, squirrels scamper and play, their bushy tails flicking back and forth as they chase each other through the undergrowth.

For those who appreciate the simple joys of life on Earth, the streams are a reminder of the beauty and tranquillity that can be found in nature. The gentle sound of water flowing over rocks, the dappled sunlight filtering through the leaves, the cool breeze that dances along the surface - all of these things combine to create a sense of peace and contentment that is unmatched by any man-made creation.

And for wildlife enthusiasts, the streams are a living testament to the resilience and adaptability of the creatures that call this place home. From the tiny insects that flit and buzz above the water to the majestic deer that come to drink at its edge, each animal plays a vital role in the delicate balance of this ecosystem.

So come, sit by the side of the stream, and let its beauty wash over you. Take a moment to appreciate the wonders of the natural world and the creatures that inhabit it. And remember, in the serenity of the streams, we can find a connection to something greater than ourselves - a connection to the earth and all its inhabitants.

The Snow Leopards

In the rugged, icy peaks of the Himalayas,
The elusive snow leopards roam,
Majestic creatures with fur like silver,
In their mountainous, snowy home.

With stealth and grace, they prowl the cliffs,
Their golden eyes keen and bright,
Adapted to the harsh, cold environment,
Surviving in the harshest of light.

Their thick coats protect them from the chill,
As they navigate the treacherous terrain,
Silent hunters, they stalk their prey,
A sight both thrilling and arcane.

These beautiful cats, so rare and wild,
Inspire awe and admiration,
Their presence a reminder of the delicate balance,
Of nature's intricate creation.

For those who glimpse them in the wild,
It's a moment to cherish and hold dear,
To witness such beauty and power,
Is to feel nature's magic near.

So let us raise our voices in praise,
Of the snow leopards' noble grace,
And vow to protect their precious habitat,
For future generations to embrace.

In the realm of the snow leopards,
Where the mountains touch the sky,
Let us honour these magnificent creatures,
And the wildness they signify.

For in their silent strength and beauty,
We find a connection to the earth,
A reminder of our place in the web of life,
And the wonder of nature's worth.

So let us celebrate the snow leopards,
In all their splendour and might,
And strive to protect their home,
In the shimmering, snowy light.

The Enchanting Elephants

In the vast savannas of Africa, there roam majestic creatures that captivate the hearts of all who behold them - the enchanting elephants. These gentle giants, with their wise eyes and graceful movements, have long been revered in folklore and poetry for their intelligence, strength, and beauty.

In the realm of nature-inspired animal poetry, the elephants hold a special place, symbolizing resilience, and harmony in the wild. Their large ears act as fans, cooling them under the scorching sun, while their powerful trunks can uproot trees and delicately pluck leaves from branches.

But it's not just their physical prowess that makes elephants so enchanting - it's also their playful and social nature. Observing a herd of elephants in the wild is like witnessing a close-knit community, where they communicate through low rumbles and gentle touches, showing love and compassion for one another. This camaraderie among elephants inspires poets to celebrate the beauty of friendship and loyalty in the animal kingdom.

In humorous animal poetry, elephants are often portrayed in whimsical scenarios, like trying to balance on a tiny stool or playing a game of hide-and-seek with mischievous monkeys. These playful depictions remind us that even the largest and most powerful creatures have a softer, more light-hearted side.

The enchanting elephants, symbols of strength, wisdom, and unity in the wild. May their presence in our world serve as a reminder of the beauty and diversity of life on Earth, inspiring us to cherish and protect all creatures, great and small.

The Elegant Giraffe

In the vast African savannah, a creature of grace and height roams free, showcasing its unique beauty with every step it takes. The elegant giraffe, with its long neck and patterned coat, is a sight to behold for any animal lover or wildlife enthusiast.

Standing tall against the backdrop of the golden sunset, the giraffe is a symbol of the beauty and wonder of the natural world. Its long eyelashes flutter in the breeze as it delicately nibbles on the leaves of the acacia tree, a picture of serenity and elegance.

In the world of animal poetry, the giraffe holds a special place. Its long legs and graceful movements inspire poets to capture its essence in verse, celebrating its unique characteristics and the role it plays in the ecosystem.

But the giraffe is not just a symbol of beauty; it is also a source of humour and joy. With its quirky appearance and gentle demeanour, this tall creature never fails to bring a smile to the faces of those who encounter it in the wild.

A true marvel of the natural world. Let us celebrate its beauty and grace through poetry, capturing the essence of this majestic animal for generations to come. For in the heart of every animal lover lies a deep appreciation for the wonders of life on Earth, embodied in the elegant giraffe.

The Majestic Tiger

In the heart of the jungle, where the trees reach for the sky and the rivers flow with a gentle murmur, there lies a creature of unparalleled beauty and grace - the majestic tiger. With its striking orange coat and dark, piercing eyes, the tiger is a sight to behold, a symbol of power and strength in the wild.

In the world of animal poetry, few creatures inspire as much awe and admiration as the tiger. Poets have long sought to capture the essence of this magnificent beast in verse, celebrating its beauty, its ferocity, and its place in the natural world.

From the humorous antics of tiger cubs at play to the solemn dignity of a mother tigress with her cubs, the tiger has provided endless inspiration for poets and writers alike. Its presence in the wild is a reminder of the delicate balance of nature, of the interconnectedness of all living things on this earth.

For animal lovers and wildlife enthusiasts, the tiger holds a special place in our hearts. We are drawn to its beauty, its power, and its mystery, and we are inspired to protect and preserve this amazing creature for future generations to enjoy.

The majestic tiger, a symbol of the beauty and wonder of the natural world. Let us honour this magnificent beast with our words and our actions, ensuring that it continues to roam the wilds of the jungle for years to come.

The Arctic Fox

The Arctic Fox is a creature of mystery and beauty, blending seamlessly into its icy surroundings with its pristine white coat. This elusive animal is a master of survival in one of the harshest environments on earth, the Arctic tundra. Its keen senses and agile movements help it navigate through the snow-covered landscape with ease, hunting for its next meal.

The Arctic Fox symbolizes resilience and adaptability, traits that are essential for life in the unforgiving Arctic wilderness.

Through humour and heartwarming verses, we explore the world of the Arctic Fox and its interactions with other creatures in its habitat. From the playful romps in the snow to the intense moments of survival against predators, the Arctic Fox's life is filled with moments of both joy and danger.

For animal lovers, life on earth enthusiasts, and wildlife enthusiasts, the Arctic Fox holds a special place in our hearts. Its beauty and grace remind us of the delicate balance of nature and the importance of preserving our precious wildlife for future generations to enjoy.

Finding Peace in the Wilderness

In the vast expanse of the wilderness, there is a sense of peace that can only be found in the presence of nature's creatures. As animal lovers and wildlife enthusiasts, we are drawn to the beauty and tranquillity that surrounds us in the great outdoors. In these moments, we find solace in the simplicity of the natural world, away from the chaos and noise of modern life.

As we immerse ourselves in these poems, we are transported to a place where time stands still, and the worries of the world fade away. We are reminded of the simple joys of watching a squirrel scamper up a tree or listening to the rushing waters of a mountain stream. In these moments, we are reminded of the healing power of nature and the profound connection we share with all living creatures.

The Bond Between Human and Animal

The bond between human and animal is one that has existed for centuries, rooted in mutual respect, love, and understanding. In the natural world, animals play a crucial role in our lives, offering companionship, protection, and even healing. This bond is perhaps most evident in the relationships we form with our pets, who become cherished members of our families, offering unwavering loyalty and unconditional love.

In the wild, the connection between humans and animals is equally profound. Wildlife enthusiasts understand the importance of preserving and protecting natural habitats for the benefit of all creatures, big and small. Through conservation efforts, we can ensure that future generations will have the opportunity to experience the wonder and beauty of the natural world.

As animal lovers, we are drawn to the unique qualities and characteristics of each species, marvelling at their intelligence, resilience, and beauty. Through poetry, we can capture the essence of these magnificent creatures, celebrating their existence and honouring their place in the world.

Respecting All Living Beings

In the vast tapestry of life on Earth, every living being plays a vital role. From the tiniest insect to the mightiest elephant, each creature contributes to the balance and beauty of our world. As animal lovers, we understand the intrinsic value of all living beings and strive to treat them with the respect and compassion they deserve.

Whether you are a seasoned wildlife enthusiast or simply someone who appreciates the beauty of the natural world, these poems will touch your heart and inspire you to see the world through the eyes of our animal friends. From the haunting call of a wolf to the gentle flutter of a butterfly's wings, each poem captures the essence of a different creature, inviting you to step into their world and experience life from their perspective.

Survival of the Fittest

In the vast wilderness, where only the strongest survive, the law of the jungle reigns supreme. It is a world where every creature must fight for its place in the natural order, where only the fittest will endure. This harsh reality is a constant reminder of the delicate balance of life in the animal kingdom.

For animal lovers, witnessing the struggle for survival can be both heartbreaking and awe-inspiring. It is a testament to the resilience and adaptability of the creatures we share this planet with. From the mighty lioness hunting for her pride to the tiny hummingbird navigating vast distances on its migration journey, each animal must rely on its instincts and abilities to overcome the challenges it faces.

As wildlife enthusiasts, we are drawn to the untamed beauty of nature and the creatures that inhabit it. We marvel at the ingenuity of the animal kingdom, where every species has evolved to thrive in its unique habitat. The survival of the fittest is not just a phrase, but a way of life for these creatures, a constant battle against predators, harsh weather, and dwindling resources.

For those who appreciate the beauty and resilience of wildlife, the concept of survival of the fittest is a powerful reminder of the interconnectedness of all living things. It is a call to action to preserve and protect the delicate balance of nature, ensuring that future generations can continue to witness the wonders of the animal kingdom.

The Beauty of Ageing

In the animal kingdom, ageing is a natural and inevitable part of life. Just like humans, animals experience the passage of time and the changes that come with it. While ageing may be seen as a sign of vulnerability or decline in some cultures, in the world of wildlife, it is often celebrated as a testament to strength, resilience, and wisdom.

As animal lovers, we have the privilege of witnessing the beauty of ageing in the creatures we admire and cherish. From the graceful dance of an elderly elephant to the silver mane of a wise wolf, there is something truly captivating about the way animals age with grace and dignity.

In the wild, older animals play vital roles in their communities. They serve as leaders, mentors, and keepers of knowledge passed down through generations. Their experiences and wisdom help guide younger members of their species, ensuring the survival and well-being of the group as a whole.

As wildlife enthusiasts, we can learn valuable lessons from the beauty of ageing in the animal kingdom. We can appreciate the importance of respecting our elders, valuing their contributions, and recognizing the unique qualities that come with age. Just as every wrinkle and scar tells a story in the wild, so too do the marks of time on our own bodies and souls.

Protecting Our Wildlife

From majestic elephants to tiny insects, every species plays a crucial role in the delicate balance of our ecosystems. Unfortunately, many animals are facing threats such as habitat destruction, poaching, and climate change. It is up to us to stand up for these voiceless creatures and advocate for their protection.

Through poetry, we can express our love and admiration for the wildlife that surrounds us. By spreading awareness and inspiring action, we can make a difference in the lives of these vulnerable creatures. From the depths of the ocean to the vast savannas, every animal deserves our respect and compassion.

As wildlife enthusiasts, we have the power to make a positive impact on the world around us. By supporting conservation organizations, volunteering at wildlife sanctuaries, and making sustainable choices in our daily lives, we can help ensure a brighter future for all living beings.

Together, let us join hands and commit to protecting our wildlife for generations to come. Let our voices be heard, our actions be meaningful, and our love for animals be unwavering. In the words of the poet, let us become the guardians of the wild and the champions of all creatures, big and small.

Preserving Natural Habitats

In the vast and intricate web of life, every creature plays a vital role in maintaining the delicate balance of nature. As animal lovers, it is our responsibility to ensure that the natural habitats of these magnificent beings are preserved and protected for generations to come.

The beauty and wonder of the natural world are unparalleled, with its diverse ecosystems and unique species that have evolved over millions of years. From the depths of the oceans to the heights of the mountains, every corner of our planet is teeming with life, each species contributing to the rich tapestry of biodiversity.

However, human activities such as deforestation, pollution, and climate change are threatening the very existence of these precious habitats. As wildlife enthusiasts, we must take action to safeguard these ecosystems and the creatures that call them home.

Through conservation efforts, we can help protect the natural habitats of animals and ensure their survival in the face of mounting threats. By supporting organizations that work to preserve these ecosystems, volunteering our time, or simply spreading awareness about the importance of conservation, we can make a difference in the fight to save our planet's wildlife.

Let us come together as animal lovers and advocates for the natural world, united in our commitment to preserving the habitats that sustain life on Earth. Through our collective efforts, we can ensure that future generations have the opportunity to experience the awe and wonder of the wild, and that our planet's diverse array of species can thrive in their natural homes.

Together, we can make a difference. Let us stand up for the voiceless creatures of the wild and work tirelessly to protect their homes and ensure a brighter future for all living beings.

Educating the Next Generation

Through the power of poetry, we can convey the wonders of the natural world in a way that captivates the imagination and stirs the soul. Poems about animals can inspire children to see beyond the surface and appreciate the unique qualities of each species. From the graceful movements of a deer to the majestic presence of a lion, our words can paint vivid pictures that ignite a passion for wildlife in young hearts.

By nurturing a love for animals early on, we can help shape future generations of conservationists and advocates for the protection of our planet's precious biodiversity. Encouraging children to observe and learn about wildlife in their natural habitats can foster a deep connection to the world around them and instil a sense of responsibility for its preservation.

Whether through reading poetry aloud, exploring nature trails, or engaging in hands-on activities that promote environmental awareness, there are endless ways to educate and inspire the next generation of animal lovers. By sowing the seeds of compassion and respect for all living beings, we can ensure a brighter future for wildlife and the natural world as a whole.

Embracing the Wild Within

In a world where we are constantly surrounded by technology and concrete jungles, it is easy to forget the wildness that lies within each of us. But as animal lovers, we understand the importance of reconnecting with our primal instincts and embracing the untamed spirit that resides in all of us.

In this subchapter, we explore the beauty and power of embracing the wild within. Just like the animals we admire and adore; we too have a fierce and untamed side that is waiting to be unleashed.

For the general public and wildlife enthusiasts alike, these poems serve as a powerful reminder of the importance of connecting with nature and honouring the wild creatures that share our planet.

So let us open our hearts to the call of the wild and embrace the untamed spirit that resides within each of us. For in doing so, we not only honour the animals that inspire us, but also awaken a sense of wonder and awe that can transform our lives in profound and meaningful ways.

The Lazy Lizard

In the heart of the jungle, where the sun beats down,
There lives a creature who wears a lazy frown.
The Lazy Lizard, with scales of green,
Is the laziest reptile that you've ever seen.

He lounges in the sun, his eyes half-closed,
Dreaming of flies and insects he's dozed.
With nothing to do but bask in the heat,
The Lazy Lizard's life is oh so sweet.

While others scurry and hunt for their food,
The Lazy Lizard is in a lazy mood.
He watches as monkeys swing from the trees,
But he'd rather just lie there and do as he please.

His friends all laugh and call him a sloth,
But the Lazy Lizard just shrugs them off.
For he knows that life is too short to be rushed,
And he's perfectly content to be hushed.

So, if you ever find yourself feeling stressed,
Just think of the Lazy Lizard at rest.
For sometimes it's best to slow down and unwind,
And let your worries slip away from your mind.

In the world of wild animals, where chaos reigns,
The Lazy Lizard knows that peace remains.

The Graceful Zebra

In the heart of the African savannah, there roams a creature so unique and stunning, it captures the imagination of all who behold it. This creature is none other than the graceful zebra, with its black and white stripes standing out against the golden grasslands.

From its sleek coat of stripes that dazzle in the sunlight to its gentle gait as it moves across the plains, the zebra is truly a sight to behold. With each step, it dances with grace and poise, a symbol of beauty in the wild.

The Mysterious Jaguar

In the heart of the dense jungle, where shadows dance and whispers linger, there lurks a creature both feared and revered - the mysterious jaguar. With its sleek coat of gold and black, eyes that gleam like orbs of fire, the jaguar prowls through the tangled vines, a silent predator in the night.

But beneath its fearsome exterior lies a creature of beauty and grace, a symbol of strength and resilience in the face of adversity. In the poem, the jaguar is portrayed as a mysterious and elusive being, a creature of mystery and intrigue that captivates the imagination of all who encounter it.

The Nosy Anteater

In the depths of the jungle, where the trees grow tall,
Lives a creature who's known for being quite nosy
overall.
The Anteater is his name, with a snout so long and thin,
He's always poking around, trying to see what's within.

With his eyes wide open and his ears perked up high,
The Anteater scours the jungle, looking for things to spy.
He's not content to just sit back and relax,
He's always on the move, searching for the facts.

If you see him coming towards you, better watch out,
He's not one to be trifled with, there's no doubt.
His curiosity knows no bounds, he'll stick his nose in your
business,
But don't worry, he means no harm, he's just a litlle
mischievous.

So, if you ever find yourself in the jungle one day,
And you spot the Anteater coming your way,
Just smile and wave, and let him do his thing,
For he's just a curious creature, with a love for exploring.

In the world of wild animals, he's quite the character,
The nosy Anteater, a true jungle adventurer.
And though he may be a little bit of a pest,
You can't help but admire his relentless quest.

The Busy Beaver

In the heart of the jungle, where the wild things roam,
There lived a beaver who always felt at home.
With a slap of his tail and a gnash of his teeth,
He worked all day, never taking a breather or a brief.

The Busy Beaver, as he was known,
Was always on the go, never alone.
Building dams and crafting homes,
He never stopped, no matter where he roamed.

His work ethic was renowned far and wide,
For he never shied away from the tide.
Chopping down trees with precision and grace,
He was truly a marvel to behold in this vast space.

But despite his busy schedule and hectic pace,
The Busy Beaver always had a smile on his face.
For he knew that his hard work would pay off in the end,
And his dedication to his craft would never bend.

So, if you ever find yourself feeling down,
Just think of the Busy Beaver, wearing his crown.
For even in the midst of chaos and strife,
There's always a lesson to be learned from this wild
animal's life.

The Roaring Tiger

In the depths of the jungle, where the trees aren't small,
Lives a creature mighty, the fiercest of them all,
With stripes of orange and eyes that gleam,
The roaring tiger, ruler of the jungle, supreme,

With a mighty roar that shakes the earth,
The tiger proclaims its royal worth,
Its power and strength unmatched by any,
In the jungle, it reigns as king, so uncanny,

In the dead of night, when the moon is bright,
The tiger prowls, its eyes alight,
Searching for prey, with stealth and grace,
Its movements silent, like a shadowy trace,

But do not be fooled by its fearsome roar,
For the tiger is more than just a predator, for sure,
Its beauty and grace, a sight to behold,
In the jungle, a creature both fierce and bold,

So let us raise a toast to the roaring tiger,
A creature of legend, a fearsome striker,
In the wilds of the jungle, it roams free,
The king of beasts, for all to see,

We celebrate the majesty of the roaring tiger,
A creature of wonder, a sight to inspire,
For poetry lovers and fans of wild animals alike,
The tiger's roar will forever strike.

The Slithering Snake

In the heart of the jungle, where the leaves rustle and the vines entwine, there lived a sly and cunning snake. With scales as dark as night and eyes that gleamed like emeralds, this serpent was feared by all who crossed its path.

But despite its fearsome reputation, the snake had a secret talent - it could recite poetry with a hiss and a slither. Its verses were filled with wit and charm, captivating all who listened to it with its clever wordplay and lyrical flair.

As the snake slithered through the jungle, it would regale the other animals with its rhymes, weaving tales of adventure and mischief that left them in stitches. From the cheeky monkeys swinging in the trees to the majestic lions prowling in the grass, everyone was enchanted by the snake's poetic prowess.

But beware, for the snake's words were not always what they seemed. Behind its playful verses lurked a cunning mind, always ready to outsmart its audience with a clever twist or a mischievous rhyme.

So, if you ever find yourself wandering through the jungle and hear a soft hiss in the undergrowth, be sure to listen closely. You may just find yourself face to face with "The Slithering Snake," the master of wild animal poetry and a true wordsmith of the jungle.

The Prowling Panther

In the heart of the jungle, where shadows dance and whispers echo, prowls the mighty panther, sleek and black as night. With eyes that gleam like glowing embers and a silent grace that sends shivers down your spine, this elusive predator rules the darkness with unmatched skill.

Through the tangled undergrowth and moonlit glades, the panther stalks its prey, a ghostly figure in the moonlight. Its velvet paws tread lightly on the forest floor, leaving no trace of its presence except for the rustle of leaves and the beating of its wild heart.

In the depths of the night, when the world is hushed and still, the panther's roar shatters the silence, a primal symphony that echoes through the trees. It is a sound that strikes fear into the hearts of all who hear it, a reminder of the raw power and untamed beauty of the jungle's most fearsome creature.

So let us raise our voices in tribute to the prowling panther, to the wild spirit that roams the shadows and the untamed heart that beats within us all. May we find inspiration in its fierce beauty and remember that in the depths of the jungle, anything is possible.

The Creepy Tarantula Spider

Hiding in the undergrowth there's a creature, relatively small;
But it's so creepy, it will make your skin crawl.
The Tarantula Spider, with its hairy legs and eyes,
Creeps up on its prey, catching them by surprise.

With fangs as sharp as needles, it strikes with great speed,
Injecting venom that makes its victims plead.
But don't be too scared, for this spider is sly,
It spins a web so sticky, it'll make you cry.

In the dead of night, when the moon is full,
The Tarantula Spider goes out on the prowl.
Silent as a whisper, it crawls through the dark,
Searching for its next meal in the jungle's park.

So, if you ever find yourself in the jungle's deep,
Beware of the Tarantula Spider as it creeps.
But don't fret too much, for it's just a little guy,
Just one of the many creatures that make the jungle alive.

So, sit back, relax, and enjoy this rhyme,
About the Creepy Tarantula Spider's creepy climb.
For in the wild, where creatures roam free,
There's always a story to tell, just like this one you see.

The Wild Tapir

In the heart of the jungle, where the trees stand tall,
Lives a creature so unique, the wildest of them all.
The tapir, with its trunk-like snout and black and white coat,
Roaming through the forest, never missing a note.

A gentle giant, with a playful demeanour,
The tapir is a sight to behold, a true jungle dreamer.
With its large ears and tiny eyes,
It moves gracefully, never telling lies.

In the depths of the jungle, where the wild things roam,
The tapir reigns supreme, making itself at home.
It munches on leaves and drinks from the streams,
Living its life as if in a dream.

Oh tapir, oh tapir, so mysterious and grand,
With your long snout and hooves in the sand.
You move with such grace and beauty untamed,
In the wild jungle, you will forever be claimed.

So let us raise a toast to this majestic beast,
Whose presence in the jungle will never cease.
For the tapir is a symbol of the wild and free,
A creature of wonder for all to see.

In the world of wild animals, the tapir stands tall,
A true masterpiece of nature, beloved by all.
So come and join us in celebrating this remarkable creature,
And let its wild spirit fill you with joy and laughter.

The Amazon Rainforest Frogs

From the vibrant, red-eyed tree frog to the elusive poison dart frog, these amphibians come in a dazzling array of colours and patterns. With their sticky tongues and bulging eyes, they are masters of camouflage and agility.

Imagine a chorus of frogs croaking in the moonlit night, their voices blending together in a symphony of sounds.

The Howling Wolf

In the heart of the jungle, where shadows dance and whispers linger, there roams a creature of mystery and might. The howling wolf, with eyes like embers and a voice that pierces the night, commands attention from all who dare to listen.

His howls are a symphony of the wild, a haunting melody that echoes through the trees and sends shivers down the spines of those who hear it. Some say he is calling to his pack; others believe he is challenging the moon itself. But one thing is certain - when the howling wolf speaks, the jungle listens.

In the realm of poetry, the howling wolf is a muse like no other. His presence evokes a sense of primal power, a reminder of the untamed spirit that resides within us all. Poets are drawn to his aura, inspired by his raw beauty and fierce independence.

The Cute Koala

In the land down under, where eucalyptus trees tower,
Lives a creature so adorable, with fur soft as a flower.
The cute koala, with its big round eyes and fluffy ears,
Brings joy to all who see it, banishing all fears.

It sleeps all day in the branches high above,
Dreaming sweet dreams of peace and love.
But when night falls and the moon is bright,
The koala awakens, ready for a midnight delight.

With a gentle smile and a playful sway,
It munches on leaves, its favourite buffet.
Its chubby cheeks and furry paws,
Make it the cutest creature you ever saw.

But don't be fooled by its innocent look,
For the koala is a master at camouflage and crook.
It may appear harmless, but it can be quite sly,
Stealing hearts with its charm, without even trying.

So next time you see a koala in a tree,
Take a moment to watch and admire its glee.
For in this wild world of jungle and tree,
The cute koala is a sight to see.

The Friendly Dolphin

In the depths of the ocean blue,
Lives a creature so friendly and true.
The dolphin, with a playful grin,
Leaps and splashes with a joyful spin.

In the vast and endless sea,
The dolphin roams so wild and free.
With a sleek and shiny form,
It dances through the waves so warm.

Its laughter echoes through the deep,
A sound that lulls the soul to sleep.
With a gentle touch and loving gaze,
The dolphin brightens up our days.

In the jungle, where the wild things play,
The dolphin swims in a graceful way.
Amongst the trees and vines so tall,
It brings a sense of peace to all.

So let us celebrate this creature so dear,
With a poem that brings it near.
The friendly dolphin, so full of grace,
Brings a smile to everyone's face.

For poetry lovers and animal fans,
This rhyme is sure to make you dance.
With humour and wit, it tells the tale,
Of the dolphin, so merry and hale.

So, raise a cheer for this majestic beast,
And let its spirit be released.
In the wild and untamed lands,
The dolphin will forever stand.

The Ferocious Great White Shark

In the deep blue sea, where the waters are dark,
Lives the mighty predator, the Great White Shark.
With rows of sharp teeth and a powerful bite,
This fearsome creature strikes fear in the night.

Its sleek, torpedo-like body cuts through the waves,
As it hunts for its prey in underwater caves.
With stealth and precision, it stalks its next meal,
Its eyes cold and black, with a hunger that's real.

But despite its reputation as a deadly foe,
The Great White Shark has a softer side, you know.
It's not all teeth and terror, as some may think,
It's just a creature trying to survive and not sink.

So, let's not judge this shark by its fearsome name,
For in the end, it's just playing nature's game.
And though it may seem scary from afar,
The Great White Shark is truly a superstar.

So, let's raise a toast to this oceanic king,
And marvel at the wonders that it can bring.
For in the world of wild animals so grand,
The Great White Shark will forever stand.

The Singing Nightingale

In the heart of the jungle, where the moon shines bright,
There lived a nightingale who sang through the night.
Her voice was melodious, sweet, and clear,
Filling the jungle with music, bringing all near.

The animals would gather around her each night,
Listening in awe to her songs, so light.
From the mighty lion to the tiny mouse,
All were captivated by her tunes, so rouse.

She sang of the stars and the shimmering moon,
Of the flowers that bloomed and the trees that swoon.
Her voice was a symphony, a true work of art,
Enchanting all who heard her, touching every heart.

The nightingale's songs were filled with magic and grace,
Transporting her listeners to a faraway place.
They would close their eyes and let her voice guide,
Through the depths of the jungle, on a mystical ride.

So, if you ever find yourself in the jungle at night,
Listen closely for the nightingale's flight.
Her songs will fill you with joy and delight,
A true masterpiece, a pure delight.

For poetry lovers and fans of wild animals,
The singing nightingale will surely enthral.
In the depths of the jungle, her voice takes flight,
A magical experience, a true delight.

The Sloth Bear

In the lush jungles of India, there roams a creature so
unique,
With shaggy fur and claws, it's a sight that's quite
mystique.
Known as the Sloth Bear, it moves with a slow pace,
But don't be fooled by its laziness, it's a force to embrace.

This curious creature, with a snout like a pig,
Is always on the hunt for some tasty fig.
With a huff and a puff, it climbs up a tree,
To feast on honeycombs, oh what a sight to see!

But beware, dear friends, of its mighty claws,
For when provoked, it's not one to pause.
With a growl and a snarl, it defends its young,
The Sloth Bear is truly wild and strong.

In the world of wild animals, it holds a special place,
For its quirky habits and gentle grace.
So let us raise a toast to the Sloth Bear,
A creature so unique and rare.

The Horned Bongo

Looking quite clumsy, like at any minute it may fall,
Lives a creature quite rare, the Horned Bongo, above all.
With stripes like a zebra and horns like a ram,
This majestic beast is truly a sight to behold, ma'am.

Its coat is a mixture of black, brown, and white,
Blending perfectly with the shadows of the night.
It moves through the undergrowth with grace,
A silent predator, on the hunt still with some pace.

But don't be fooled by its elegant gait,
The Horned Bongo is also known to be great.
At telling jokes and making others laugh,
Its sense of humour is truly top-notch, on behalf.

So, if you ever find yourself in the jungle so wild,
Keep an eye out for the Horned Bongo, styled.
With its wit and charm, it's sure to amuse,
And leave you laughing until you can't refuse.

For poetry lovers and humour enthusiasts alike,
The Horned Bongo is a creature you'll want to strike.
With its wild antics and comedic flair,
It's a true gem in the jungle, beyond compare.

The Sleepy Sloth

In the heart of the jungle, where the trees grow tall,
Lives a creature so slow, it can barely crawl.
The Sleepy Sloth, with his fur so grey,
Spends his days lounging, never in a hurry to play.

He hangs from a branch, his eyes half-closed,
Dreaming of adventures, where he's not opposed.
To moving quickly or getting things done,
But for now, he'll just soak up the sun.

The Sleepy Sloth is a sight to behold,
With his long limbs and claws so bold.
He moves with grace, though at a snail's pace,
And his smile never leaves his face.

His friends in the jungle all know him well,
For his laziness is a story they love to tell.
But deep down, they admire his easy-going ways,
And wish they could spend their days in a similar daze.

So if you ever find yourself feeling stressed and blue,
Just think of the Sleepy Sloth, and what he would do.
He'd find a comfy branch, and take a little nap,
For sometimes the best medicine is a good, long, catnap.

In the world of wild animals, he may not be the best,
But the Sleepy Sloth surely knows how to rest.
And in this hectic world we live in today,
We could all learn a little from the sleepy sloth's way.

The Mighty Green Turtle

In the lush jungles of the world, there lives a creature so grand,
With a shell on its back, it roams the land,
The mighty green turtle, so slow and serene,
In its world of green, it is the queen.

With a shell as tough as nails, it carries its home,
Through forests and rivers, it loves to roam,
Its slow and steady pace, a sight to behold,
In the wild, its story is often told.

In the midst of the jungle's wild embrace,
The green turtle finds its peaceful place,
Among the towering trees and babbling brooks,
It hides and waits in hidden nooks.

With a wise old look in its ancient eyes,
The green turtle is truly a wondrous prize,
For those who seek to understand its ways,
Will find a treasure that forever stays.

So let us raise a cheer for this noble friend,
Whose presence in the wild will never end,
The mighty green turtle, so grand and true,
In the jungle's heart, it will forever renew.

For poetry lovers and animal enthusiasts alike,
The green turtle's story is sure to strike,
A chord of laughter and wonder so true,
In the wild, where dreams come anew.

The Prickly Hedgehog

Mooching around eating bugs, and having a ball,
Lives a prickly hedgehog, both big and small.
With spiky quills that gleam in the sun,
He scurries around, always on the run.

But don't be fooled by his prickly exterior,
For this hedgehog is quite the interior decorator.
His burrow is cozy, filled with treasures untold,
Like shiny rocks and leaves of gold.

He's a master of camouflage, blending in with the trees,
No one can spot him, not even the bees.
But if you listen closely, you might hear his snore,
As he dreams of adventures, galore.

The hedgehog is a creature of mystery and charm,
With a personality that's full of alarm.
But don't let his prickly nature scare you away,
For deep down, he's just looking for a friend to play.

So next time you're wandering through the jungle so wild,
Keep an eye out for the hedgehog, both big and mild.
And if you're lucky enough to catch a glimpse of his
quills,
You'll know you've witnessed one of nature's greatest
thrills.

The Curious Sealion

In the depths of the ocean blue,
Lives a sealion with a curious view.
Always poking its nose where it doesn't belong,
This playful creature can never go wrong.

With whiskers like a cat and a bark like a dog,
The sealion roams the ocean like a playful log.
It flips and flops with grace so fine,
Capturing the hearts of those who dine.

Its eyes sparkle with mischief and glee,
As it dives and dances in the sea.
Curiosity drives its every move,
Exploring the depths with nothing to prove.

From the kelp forests to the sandy shore,
The sealions adventures are never a bore.
It chases fish and plays with its friends,
Making sure the fun never ends.

So, if you ever spot a sealion at play,
Take a moment to watch and stay.
For in its antics and curious ways,
You'll find joy that brightens your days.

The Curious Sealion is a creature so rare,
With a spirit that's beyond compare.
So let its story fill you with delight,
And keep the wonder alive both day and night.

For in the wild and untamed sea,
The sealion roams wild and free.
And in its curious and playful way,
It reminds us to live and enjoy each day.

The Peru Lama

In the lush jungles of Peru, there roams a creature so rare and majestic, it is almost like something out of a dream. The Peru lama is a unique and fascinating animal that captivates all who are lucky enough to catch a glimpse of it.

With its long, flowing coat of fur and graceful movements, the Peru lama is a sight to behold. It is said to possess a sense of wisdom and serenity that is unmatched by any other creature in the jungle. Its eyes are deep and soulful, reflecting the ancient knowledge of the land in which it roams.

In the world of wild animal poetry, the Peru lama holds a special place. Poets have been inspired by its beauty and grace, crafting verses that capture the essence of this magnificent creature. From its gentle demeanour to its mysterious ways, the Peru Lama is a muse for poets seeking to explore the wonders of the natural world.

The Fruit Bat

In the depths of the jungle, hanging upside down,
Is a creature quite unique, with a furry brown gown.
The fruit bat is its name, a winged wonder to behold,
With a face only a mother could love, or so we are told.

With eyes like shiny marbles and ears like radar dishes,
This nocturnal creature feasts on fruits and makes many
wishes.
Flying through the night with grace and skill,
The fruit bat is a master of the air, never standing still.

In the canopy of trees, it makes its home,
Singing sweet songs as it roams and roams.
Its wingspan wide, its flight a sight to see,
The fruit bat is truly wild and free.

So, if you ever find yourself in the jungle so grand,
Look up in the sky and you might just understand,
The beauty of the fruit bat, with its wings spread wide,
A creature of the night, with nothing to hide.

This poem is dedicated to all the fruit bats out there,
Flying through the jungle without a single care.
May your wings always be strong, your fruit always
sweet,
And may you never lose your sense of wonder and treat.

The Games They Play

Up and down, in and out,
Round and round, all about,
Jumping and leaping,
Searching for food,
Then burying some,
For a later date,
Scurrying about,
At such great speed,
Is there really, such a need,
Or is it simply, purely just greed?
Forever on the move,
Never still, for very long,
Like they have something to prove,
Darting, from tree to tree,
So funny, to watch and see,
A squirrel, chasing its competitors away,
Or is this just, the games they play?

Cyril the Squirrel

There's a friendly squirrel called Cyril,
Who lives in a tree, in a park on the Wirral,
He scavenges for food from the bins, at the back of Lidl,

He scampers up and down, the bark of a tree,
Skipping from branch to branch, with such ease,
It doesn't take much, for him to be pleased,

With his whiskers, and a big fluffy tail,
He sits and watches curiously, at a slow-moving snail,
As it slithers along, a cold metal rail,

He is friends with all the mice, foxes, and bats,
He likes kind people, some wearing bright coloured hats,
Although he's not so keen, on the big smelly rats,

Cyril's quite scarred of hedgehogs, cats, and big dogs,
He's bemused by the woodlice, munching on logs;
And strange looking, small slimy green frogs,

Cyril likes humans, as they feed him monkey nuts and
bread rolls;
But he runs away, from furry wee moles,
Every time they pop their heads, out of their holes,

Only Cyril the squirrel, knows what life really means,
Always picturing acorns and nuts, in his dreams,
Life's pretty simple for Cyril, so it seems.

The Real Angry Birds

The real angry birds,
Quite aggressive and mean,
Ten-inch terrors,
They nest in crevices,
Within holes in the cliffs,
Some up to a metre deep,
With white bellies, and orange beaks,
Black bodies and little red feet,
The puffin, so beautiful and sweet,
Something you really, should go and see.

Frogs Everywhere

Watching as frogs start emerging, from a small pond,
You can see why people like them, and become quite
fond,

They jump about, all covered in slime,
Pairing up in two's, when it's mating time,

All slippery and wet, living life in the wild,
The weather quite nice, and pretty mild,

Before long, I had to watch where I stood,
Standing and walking, wherever I could,

The grassy ground, was covered in frogs,
Now all marshy, more like a bog,

Frogs everywhere, one on top of the other,
To produce spawn, then become fathers and mothers.

Pine Marten

Pine marten, sleek and long,
Belly to the ground, as they sneak along,

An elusive, furry wild animal,
Such a beautiful, fast moving wee mammal,

Birds of prey, patrol the skies and rove,
Hills of wild heather, with flowers of mauve,

Rabbits and hare, chased by wild feral cats,
Or tasty snacks, like field mice and rats,

Wild deer, timidly roam by,
Eating grasses and plants, always so shy,

Natural ponds, with reeds and bulrushes,
Buzzard's overhead, with magpies and thrushes,

Frogs in droves, come mating time,
The chorus of croaks, covered in slime.

Songs of the Birds

In the tranquil realm of nature's melodies, the songs of the birds reign supreme. Their sweet trills and joyful chirps fill the air with a symphony of sound that captivates the soul and stirs the heart.

From the haunting call of the loon to the cheerful warble of the robin, each bird has its own unique voice that adds to the tapestry of nature's chorus.

Take a moment to immerse yourself in the world of the birds, to listen to their songs and feel their presence all around you.

Whispers of the Trees

In the heart of the forest, where the trees stand tall and proud, there is a symphony of whispers that only the keenest ears can hear. The rustling of leaves, the creaking of branches, the gentle swaying of the canopy above – all of these sounds come together to form a chorus of nature's own making.

For the poetry lovers who find solace in the natural world, these whispers of the trees are like music to their souls. They speak of ancient wisdom, of secrets long forgotten, of stories that have been passed down through generations. Each tree has its own tale to tell, its own voice to contribute to the symphony of the forest.

As we walk through the woods, we can feel the energy of the trees around us. They are alive and vibrant, pulsing with the rhythms of the earth. They are home to countless creatures, from tiny insects to majestic birds of prey, all of whom find shelter and sustenance in their branches.

In the world of animal and wildlife poetry, the trees play a central role. They are the backdrop against which the dramas of the natural world unfold. They are the silent witnesses to the struggles and triumphs of the creatures that inhabit the forest.

So let us pause for a moment, dear poetry lovers, and listen to the whispers of the trees. Let us allow their voices to inspire us, to guide us, to remind us of the beauty and wonder of the natural world. For in their whispers, we can find solace, wisdom, and a connection to something greater than ourselves.

Howls of the Wolves

In the dead of night, when the moon is bright,
The haunting howls of the wolves fill the air,
A symphony of wilderness, raw and rare,
Echoing through the forest, a primal delight.

Poetry lovers, gather 'round,
For a tale of the creatures that roam the wild,
Their voices fierce, yet strangely mild,
Their presence leaving an eerie sound.

The wolves, majestic and free,
Their howls speak of ancient lands,
Of hunts and packs and shifting sands,
A glimpse of nature's harmony.

Their voices carry across the plains,
A language of the untamed,
A melody that cannot be named,
A song that soothes and entertains.

So listen closely, poetry lovers,
To the howls of the wolves in the night,
For in their wild and untamed cries,
You'll find a beauty like no other.

For in the heart of the wilderness,
Where the moon shines bright and the stars are near,
The howls of the wolves will always be clear,
A reminder of nature's perfectness.

Haikus for the Butterflies

In the world of nature's creatures, butterflies hold a special place with their delicate beauty and graceful fluttering wings. These enchanting insects inspire poets and artists alike with their vibrant colours and ephemeral presence. In this subchapter, we explore the beauty of butterflies through the ancient art of haiku poetry.

Gentle wings take flight
Butterflies dance in the light
Nature's pure delight

Each haiku in this collection captures a moment of wonder and awe as we observe these winged wonders in their natural habitat. From the monarch's majestic migration to the swallowtail's intricate patterns, each butterfly is a work of art in motion.

Fluttering free
Butterflies kiss flowers sweetly
Nature's harmony

As poetry lovers, we are drawn to the beauty and simplicity of haiku, a form of Japanese poetry that captures the essence of a moment in just a few short lines. Through haiku, we can connect with the natural world and appreciate the fleeting beauty of butterflies as they flit and flutter through our gardens and meadows.

Butterflies in flight
Whisper secrets of the night
Nature's pure delight

Join us on a journey through the world of butterflies, where words and images intertwine to create a tapestry of beauty and wonder. Through haiku poetry, we can celebrate the delicate and ephemeral beauty of these enchanting creatures and find inspiration in their graceful dance through the air.

Mountain Goats

In the craggy cliffs where the mountain goats roam,
Their nimble hooves find a sure-footed home.
High above the valleys, they stand proud and free,
A sight to behold for all who can see.

Their coats are white as freshly fallen snow,
Blending in with the peaks where they go.
With horns that curl like the crescent moon,
They navigate the rocks with grace and tune.

Their eyes are keen, their senses sharp,
Guided by instinct, they never depart.
They leap and bound with effortless ease,
A dance of nature among the trees.

Oh, mountain goats, so wild and bold,
Your beauty a story waiting to be told.
In the rugged terrain where you make your abode,
You inspire us with your fearless ode.

So let us raise our voices high,
In praise of these creatures that touch the sky.
May their spirits forever soar,
In the wild verses we adore.

For poetry lovers who seek the sublime,
The mountain goats are a symbol of time.
Their resilience and strength a lesson to learn,
In the wild verses where we yearn.

The Mountain Lion

In the heart of the mountains, where the shadows dance,
There roams a creature, fierce and free, in a wild trance.
The mountain lion, with eyes like embers, prowls with grace,
A silent predator in this untamed place.

Oh, noble beast, with strength and stealth,
Your presence in these rugged lands is like a wealth.
Your golden coat, your sinewy form,
A testament to nature's power and charm.

In the stillness of the night, you move like a ghost,
Through rocky crags and forests, you are the host.
Your primal instinct, your primal call,
Echoes through the mountains, standing tall.

Oh, mountain lion, fearsome and bold,
You are a legend, a story untold.
Your eyes hold secrets of ancient lore,
Of battles fought and territories to explore.

So let us raise our voices in tribute to thee,
Oh mighty mountain lion, wild and free.
May your spirit forever roam these lands,
A symbol of nature's strength and grandeur, so grand.

In the world of poetry, where words take flight,
Let us honour the mountain lion with all our might.
For in its eyes, we see the wild and untamed,
A creature of beauty, forever unnamed.

For poetry lovers and those who adore
The beauty of nature, the wild's grandeur and more,
These verses for the mountain lion are a call
To appreciate and cherish nature's creatures, big and small.

Tributes to the Elephants

In the vast savannas of Africa,
Where the giants roam free,
We pay homage to the majestic elephants,
Symbols of strength and grace in the wild.

Their tusks gleam in the sunlight,
A reminder of their noble heritage,
Passed down through generations,
A legacy of resilience and power.

Poetry lovers, gather 'round,
Listen to the tales of these gentle giants,
Whose presence commands respect,
Whose beauty inspires awe.

Their trumpeting calls echo through the plains,
A symphony of nature's grandeur,
A language of love and family,
A bond that transcends time.

In the shadows of the acacia trees,
We watch as they move with grace,
Their footsteps leaving imprints,
In the soft earth beneath their feet.

Oh, how we marvel at their intelligence,
Their empathy and compassion,
Their wisdom that surpasses our own,
In the ways of the wild.

So let us raise our voices in tribute,
To the elephants of the savanna,
To their strength and their beauty,
To their place in the tapestry of life.

For in their presence, we find solace,
In their eyes, we see a reflection,
Of the wildness within us all,
A reminder of our connection to the earth.

So let us honour these gentle giants,
In our words and in our hearts,
For they are the guardians of the wild,
And the keepers of nature's secrets.

Black-Faced Sheep

Hiking up, and over the hills,
Seeing such a landscape, always thrills,

Following well-worn paths and tracks,
Passing derelict old barns, and crumbling shacks,

Wildlife roaming, free and wild,
The weather mostly, dry, and mild,

Fields as green, as a pool table baize,
As the black-faced sheep wander and graze,

Flowing hills, rise into the sky,
Looking up, to see majestic birds fly,

Breathing in, the clean, fresh air,
They'll always be something, to make you stare,

Wandering along, without a worry or a care,
The views are free, and it's all there to share.

Flittering and Fluttering

Hawthorn and brambles,
With berries, plump and ripe,
All shades of red, blue, and black,
Growing freely, such a delight,
Foxgloves, and giant daisies,
Wild orchids, and poppies, too,
The sun shining brightly,
The view becomes quite hazy,
So many plants, fresh and new,
Flowers all on show
With petals so bright,
Where pollen does flow,
So clearly in sight,
Birds, bees, and insects,
Chirp, sing and whistle,
Their usual sweet tune,
Humming and swooping,
Flittering and fluttering,
Picking and pecking,
As they crawl and buzz,
Scrambling for dear life,
Feeding with all their might,
Before autumn sets in,
When food becomes tight,
Every day is a battle;
Just to stay alive.

Pheasants Roaming

The early morning mist, so new,
Spider webs, covered in morning dew,

Birds build their nests, with straw and twigs,
As a farmer feeds, his chickens and pigs,

Pheasants roaming, in the fields so wild,
With the weather, cool but still quite mild,

The countryside, always so elegant and serene,
Most of the year, it's all dark green,

Flower buds opening, petals bright and glowing,
With a gentle, mild breeze, steadily blowing,

Honeybees buzzing, even in a light shower,
Fluttering and scurrying, from flower to flower,

In the summer, landscapes are scenic and unique;
But in the winter, they're pretty cold, harsh, and bleak.

Seagulls Screeching

Peace and quiet, along the shores,
The beauty of heather, growing wild on the moors,

Seagulls screeching, while flying high above,
Swans glide by in groups, of family love,

Tides go in and out, twice every day,
To see these scenes, we have nothing to pay,

Rugged rocks, hills, castles and more,
Views that makes life, worth living for,

The Scottish coastline, is one to behold,
More precious and beautiful, than even pure gold,

Heaven on Earth, if the truth is to be told,
Glorious, serene, and ever so old.

The Birds and the Bees

Fields being ploughed,
Seeds soon to be sewn,
Where plants and crops,
Are nurtured and grown,

The birds and the bees,
Fly, swarm and roam,
Rabbits digging up veggies,
Growing In rows,

Gardens, full of fresh flowers,
In bloom, and on show,
The air, full of scent,
Such fragrant, sweet smells.

Dancing Birds, Shuffling Feet

Flawless nature, such a treat,
Dancing birds, shuffling feet,

Hawthorns and brambles, where berries grow,
The birds when hungry, know where to go,

Flower petals, blow in the breeze,
Woodlands and forests, full of pine trees,

Wild grasses and plants, flow, and sway,
It's that time of year, for baling hay,

All rolled up in bales, ever so neat,
Left out to dry, in the summer heat.

Honeybees Roam

The haze, from the morning mist,

Dew making wild blackberries, shine, and glisten,

The twice-daily tides, lash along the shore,

Where pipistrelle bats, fly at twilight,

Wild orchids grow, in the untouched fields,

Embankments, full of large poppies and daisies,

Butterflies, birds, and honeybee's roam,

Swooping and flying, from bud to bud,

Bushes, brambles, long grasses, and trees,

Scenic views, which do nothing but please,

Nature's beauty is more like a glorious dream.

The Birds Fly and Sing

Walking through, the morning breeze,
Admiring the birds, the flora, and trees,

Looking at flowers, and busy bees,
Things I wish, and love to see,

Trampling through, the woods and fields,
Kicking up, piles of leaves,

The Glens in view, as I walk by,
Climbing over, the occasional sty,

The birds fly and sing, in the sky,
Fluffy clouds, floating way up high,

Walking in the hills, with blue skies above,
Seeing wild animals, those that we all love,

Mooching through, the long-wet grass,
Sheep in the fields, as I pass,

Seeing horses, running freely at play,
Walking past fields, stacked with bales of hay,

True beauty never fails, to please,
It reminds me of how life should be.

Buzzards Flying Over

The stunning, hills and glens,

With their, fantastic wild splendour,

It doesn't matter, who you are,

Or your race, age, or gender,

Beauty is beauty; at the end of the day,

Nature provides, all this for free,

Beautiful memories, we always remember,

Even if, the weather's not great,

The moorland, with wild heather,

Rolling hills, with their flowing grace,

Buzzard's flying over, with such majestic pace,

The wildlife on show is always such a pleasure to see.

Grey Seals

Vast sandy beaches,
High treacherous cliffs,

Scotland's ancient past,
The legends, mysteries, and myths,

Coastal paths, new and old,
Grasses, rocks, vast and bold,

Sand dunes, hills, and mountains,
Otherworldly landscapes, untold,

Grey seals on the coastline, and shores,
Sea life in abundance, in our seas,

Creatures living on the seabed floor,
Vast arrays of species, never displease.

Small Crabs Hide and Dwell

The sea lashes, along the shores,
Saltwater, always flows and pours,

It ripples, in the Scottish sands,
In these stunning, coastal lands,

Rocks, pebbles, and sunny spells,
Washed up, occasionally pretty shells,

Tiny fish, caught in small rock pools,
Usually full of life, as a rule,

Where small crabs, hide and dwell,
With all the usual, seaside smell,

Taking a stroll, along the beach,
There is so much enjoyment, and it is always within
reach.

Pipistrelle Bats

Bees busily buzzing, collecting pollen;

It's their daily toil, a lifelong plight,

Ladybirds, fly and crawl;

Always so cute, small, and light,

Dragonflies, glide around;

Catching bugs, in mid-flight,

If horseflies land, on your skin,

They will give you, a nasty bite,

Butterflies, flapping and fluttering;

Their majestic wings, with all their might,

Pipistrelle bats, come out to hunt and fly;

As they feed, during the night,

Birds are great, aerial masters;

In the sky, so dominant at great
height.

Dragonflies Swoop

Dragonflies, swoop, and fly,
Looping the loop, low and high,

In a pond, with fish below,
Ducks on the top following, wherever they go,

Bugs and flies, swarm on mass,
Frogs venture out onto the grass,

Butterflies land, on flowers in bloom,
For all these creatures, there's plenty of room,

Wasps, bees, low-hanging trees,
Dandelions, sitting pretty in the breeze,

Stinging nettles, growing wild,
Spring and summer months, warm and mild,

Blackberries grow, plump and ripe,
Birds aren't fussy, they'll eat all types,

Bats come out, to feed at night,
Using sonar to manoeuvre, due to poor sight.

Wild Feral Cat

The wild feral cat,

Larger than the domestic type,

All black and living wild,

Chasing a rabbit, with all its might,

Up in the hills,

Bobbing and weaving,

Scampering around,

Jumping and skipping,

In and out of the bushes,

Through the long grass,

At great speed,

Trying to catch its prey;

But the cat tires quickly;

And the rabbit, finally gets away.

Sheep and Cows in the Fields

Meandering along, a scenic country lane,
Birds still singing, in the drizzling rain,
The views all around, are stunningly insane,

Dark skies move along, to reveal clouds of pure white,
The sun starts to shine, such a welcoming sight,
A beautiful day, with a warm glow of delight,

Birds flutter from the trees, without any haste,
Fresh air circulating, that you can almost taste,
It's a view not everyone gets to see; it is such a waste,

As branches sway, this way and that,
Pinecones growing, plump and fat,
Scenes that make you smile, like the Cheshire Cat,

Leaves, all shades of green some with a yellow haze,
Sheep and cows in the fields, all peacefully graze,
Forests of pine trees all around, like an overgrown maze.

Living in the Sea

Walking through gorgeous meadows, the senses they please,
A visual treat, in a warm summer breeze,

When in mid-winter, trees covered in a layer of snow,
Experience the joys, of our nature's glow,

Scenery that brings, such joyous thrills,
Lands of lush green fields, and stunning hills,

Mountain ranges, that go on forever,
With the purple haze, of flowing wild heather,

From the blossoms that will bloom, come what may,
To the farmers busy harvesting, fresh golden hay

So many creatures, living wild and free,
With fish and so much life, living in the sea,

Don't destroy, planet Earth's natural beauty,
As an intelligent species, it's undoubtedly our duty,

Protect our planet, and nature's beautiful gifts,
There's too much destruction, from wars and rifts.

The Graceful Zebra

In the vast savannas of Africa,
A creature with stripes roams free,
Graceful and majestic, the zebra,
A sight to behold for all to see.

Its coat of black and white,
A symbol of harmony and balance,
In the wild, it's a beautiful sight,
A creature that's truly a wonder of existence.

With each step, it moves with grace,
A dance of nature in motion,
In the wild, it finds its place,
A creature that's a true devotion.

Oh, zebra with your stripes so bold,
A creature of beauty and grace,
In the wild, you never grow old,
A symbol of the Earth's embrace.

Penguins, So Sleek and Grand

In the icy lands of the South Pole,
Where snow and cold winds take their toll,
There waddle creatures black and white,
With tuxedo coats shining in the light.

Penguins, oh penguins, so sleek and grand,
Marching together across the land,
Their wings may not let them take to flight,
But in the water, they're a magnificent sight.

With flippers that propel them through the sea,
They dive and swim with grace and glee,
In search of fish and squid to eat,
Their underwater dance is truly a treat.

So let us celebrate these birds of the ice,
With their waddling gait and hearts so nice,
May we learn from them to work as a team,
And cherish the beauty of nature's dream.

Armadillo

The armadillo, with its armoured shell,
A creature of wonder, a creature of hell.
In the moonlit night, it scurries along,
A silent guardian, both fierce and strong.

Its scales gleam in the silver light,
A sight to behold, a wondrous sight.
In the depths of the forest, it roams free,
A symbol of resilience, a symbol of glee.

Oh armadillo, creature of the night,
With your armour shining so bright,
You captivate us with your grace,
A gentle soul in a rugged place.

In the realm of wildlife poetry,
The armadillo stands tall and free.
So let us celebrate this unique creature,
In all its glory and all its feature.

Secrets of the Coral Reef

Welcome to the enchanting world of the coral reef, where vibrant colours and mysterious creatures dance beneath the waves. In this subchapter, we will explore the hidden secrets of this underwater paradise through the lens of poetry, capturing the beauty and wonder of these unique ecosystems. From the delicate swaying of sea anemones to the graceful movements of schools of fish, the coral reef is a treasure trove of inspiration for poets and nature lovers alike.

As we dive deeper into the secrets of the coral reef, we are reminded of the delicate balance that exists within this intricate ecosystem. Each creature plays a vital role in maintaining the health and vitality of the reef, from the tiny coral polyps that build the reef structure to the majestic predators that hunt among its crevices. Through poetry, we can celebrate the interconnectedness of all living beings and the importance of preserving these fragile habitats for future generations to enjoy.

One of the most fascinating aspects of the coral reef is its ability to adapt and evolve in the face of changing environmental conditions. Through centuries of evolution, these resilient organisms have developed unique strategies for survival, from the symbiotic relationships between coral and algae to the camouflage techniques of elusive octopuses. By exploring these adaptations through poetry, we can gain a deeper appreciation for the ingenuity and resilience of life in the ocean.

In our exploration of the coral reef through poetry, we are also reminded of the threats that these fragile ecosystems face in the modern world. From climate change and pollution to overfishing and habitat destruction, the coral reef is under constant pressure from human activities. Through our words and our actions, we can raise awareness of these threats and work towards protecting and preserving these vital ecosystems for future generations.

In conclusion, the coral reef is a source of endless inspiration for poets and nature lovers alike, with its vibrant colours, mysterious creatures, and hidden secrets waiting to be discovered.

The Elegant Seahorse

In the depths of the ocean, where the waters are clear,
There swims a creature so graceful, so delicate, so dear.
The seahorse, with its intricate patterns and curves,
Captivates all who have the fortune to observe.

Its slender body sways with the rhythm of the tide,
As it glides through the water, with such effortless pride.
With eyes that shimmer like jewels in the sun,
The seahorse is a marvel, second to none.

In the dance of the sea, it moves with such grace,
A creature of beauty, in its rightful place.
Its tail curls like a tendril, reaching out to the sky,
As if to touch the heavens, with a gentle sigh.

Oh, seahorse, how you enchant us with your elegance,
A symbol of beauty, in a world of magnificence.
May we always treasure and protect your kind,
For in your delicate form, true beauty we find.

Jellyfish Drift

In the stillness of the ocean's embrace,
The jellyfish drifts with effortless grace.
Its tentacles trailing like ribbons of silk,
A creature of beauty, mysterious and surreal.

In the depths where light barely reaches,
The jellyfish glows with a soft luminescence.
A shimmering beacon in the darkness,
A vision of wonder, a creature of enchantment.

Its movements are like a ballet,
A dance of fluidity and elegance.
Suspended in time, it glides through the water,
A silent and graceful presence in the depths below.

In the poetry of the ocean, the jellyfish sings,
A symphony of light and shadow, of beauty and mystery.
Its delicate form a testament to nature's artistry,
A reminder of the wonders that lie beneath the surface.

The Oyster Nurtures its Pearl

In the depths of the ocean, a humble oyster lies,
With a secret so precious, hidden from prying eyes.
A pearl of pure beauty, growing slowly within,
A treasure of the sea, where only dreams begin.

The oyster feels the weight of the world on its shell,
But inside, a pearl is forming, a story to tell.
It takes patience and time for this gem to unfold,
A precious gift from nature, worth more than pure gold.

As the oyster nurtures its pearl, with love and care,
It knows that one day, it will be free to share.
For now, it remains hidden, a mystery unseen,
A symbol of hope and beauty, in a world so serene.

So let us admire the oyster, in its quiet grace,
And marvel at the wonder of this hidden place.
For within its shell, a pearl of wisdom grows,
A reminder of the beauty that nature bestows.

In the depths of the ocean, where life is so wild,
The oyster and its pearl are nature's own child.
So let us celebrate this magical sight,
And cherish the wonder of nature's delight.

Monkeys Swinging in the Trees

In the lush green forests of the world, there is a magical sight to behold - monkeys swinging in the trees. These playful creatures, with their agile bodies and nimble limbs, move through the branches with grace and ease. Their joyful antics bring a sense of wonder and delight to all who witness them.

As they swing from tree to tree, the monkeys seem to dance with the wind, their movements fluid and effortless. Their calls and chatter fill the air, creating a symphony of sound that echoes through the forest. It is a reminder of the wild and untamed beauty of nature, a world where creatures live in harmony with the earth.

Watching the monkeys in their natural habitat, one cannot help but feel a sense of connection to the world around them. These creatures, so similar to us in many ways, remind us of our shared ancestry and the importance of preserving the delicate balance of the natural world. They are a symbol of the resilience and adaptability of life, a testament to the power of evolution and the wonders of creation.

In their playful antics and curious nature, the monkeys inspire us to embrace the joy and wonder of the world around us. They remind us to take a moment to appreciate the beauty of nature, to cherish the creatures that share our planet, and to remember our place in the intricate web of life. They are a source of inspiration and wonder, a reminder of the magic and mystery that surrounds us each and every day.

Gazelle Running Wild and Free

In the vast expanse of the African savanna, the graceful gazelle runs wild and free, a symbol of beauty and freedom in the natural world. With its slender legs and elegant stride, the gazelle moves with a fluidity and grace that captivates all who witness its movements.

As the sun rises over the horizon, casting a golden glow over the savanna, the gazelle leaps into action, its hooves pounding against the earth in a rhythmic dance of life and vitality. With each bound, the gazelle seems to defy gravity, soaring through the air with a lightness and agility that is truly awe-inspiring.

In the stillness of the night, the gazelle's eyes gleam in the darkness, a beacon of light and life in the shadowy landscape. With its keen senses and sharp instincts, the gazelle is always on high alert, ready to spring into action at the first sign of danger.

As the seasons change and the landscape shifts, the gazelle adapts and thrives, its resilience and strength a testament to the enduring power of nature.

The Nosy Meerkat

In the vast plains of Africa, there lives a curious creature that never fails to capture the attention of onlookers - the meerkat. With their slender bodies, alert eyes, and distinctive upright posture, meerkats are truly fascinating animals to observe in the wild.

The Nosy Meerkat would spend hours each day scanning the horizon, searching for any signs of danger or opportunity. With its keen eyesight and sharp reflexes, it was always the first to detect any potential threats, whether it be a prowling predator or a rival meerkat encroaching on its territory. The other members of the meerkat clan relied on the Nosy Meerkat to keep them safe and informed, trusting in its ability to sniff out danger from afar.

It was also a keen observer of the natural world around it, taking delight in the beauty of the sunrise, the playfulness of the young meerkat pups, and the intricate patterns of the desert landscape. The Nosy Meerkat's observations inspired awe and wonder in its fellow clan members, who often gathered around to listen to its tales of the world beyond their burrow.

The Graceful Giraffe

In the heart of the African savannah, a majestic creature roams,
Tall and graceful, the giraffe stands proud in its home,
With a long neck reaching towards the sky,
Its spots like constellations, catching the eye,

A poem about a giraffe, so wondrous and rare,
Capturing the essence of this creature with care,
Its gentle eyes and peaceful demeanour,
A symbol of grace, a true-life streamer,

In the vast expanse of the wild, the giraffe roams free,
Its beauty and elegance a sight to see,
A creature of wonder, a creature of awe,
So magnificent, that we find a connection so raw,

So let us celebrate this creature of the earth,
In our poems and stories, giving it worth,
For the giraffe is a symbol of the wild and free,
A reminder of the beauty in nature for you and me.

The Mighty Buffalo Roam

In the heart of the prairie, the mighty buffalo roam,
With strength and grace, it wanders free, in its natural home.
A symbol of resilience, a creature of the land,
A majestic presence, so grand.

Its hooves pound the earth, stirring up dust,
A reminder of a time when they once roamed in vast herds, with trust.
Their power and beauty, unmatched by any other,
A sight to behold, a true wonder.

Through the changing seasons, the buffalo endures,
Facing challenges with courage, its spirit pure.
In harmony with nature, it thrives and survives,
A testament to the wild, where freedom thrives.

So let us honour the buffalo, in all its glory,
For it represents the untamed spirit of the prairie story.
A creature of strength, of grace, of might,
A symbol of the wild, a breathtaking sight.

Kangaroo Stands Tall

In the vast Australian outback, the kangaroo roams,
Galloping gracefully with their powerful limbs,
A symbol of freedom in the wild,
Their beauty captured in poems and songs.

Their fur a soft shade of grey,
Eyes bright with curiosity and wonder,
Kangaroos are a sight to behold,
A true marvel of the natural world.

In the quiet of the morning,
As the sun rises over the horizon,
The kangaroo stands tall and proud,
A testament to the resilience of nature.

Their gentle hopping echoes through the bush,
A rhythmic beat that resonates with the earth,
In the kangaroo, we find a connection,
To the wild and untamed spirit within us all.

So let us celebrate these magnificent creatures,
With words that capture their essence,

You can't help but to adore the kangaroo,
And all the creatures that share our beautiful planet.

Haiku about the Badger

In the quiet of the forest, the badger emerges from its burrow, a creature of mystery and grace. Haiku poems about the badger capture the essence of this elusive animal, its solitary nature and fierce determination. These short, powerful verses offer a glimpse into the world of the badger, inviting readers to contemplate its place in the natural world.

In the darkness of night
the badger prowls silently
a shadow in the moonlight

With claws sharp as knives
it digs deep into the earth
seeking hidden treasures

In the stillness of dawn
the badger rests in its den
dreaming of the hunt

Through fields of green grass
the badger roams freely
a ghost in the daylight

In the hush of twilight
the badger disappears
a phantom in the shadows

Haiku poems about the badger capture the essence of this enigmatic creature, its strength and resilience in the face of adversity. These short, evocative verses speak to the heart of the wilderness, reminding us of the interconnectedness of all living things. For poetry readers and wildlife enthusiasts alike, the badger remains a symbol of the untamed beauty of the natural world, a creature to be revered and respected.

Haiku about the Otter

Haiku poems about otters capture the playful and curious nature of these enchanting creatures. Otters are known for their graceful movements in the water and their adorable antics on land. In just a few short lines, haiku poems can beautifully convey the essence of otters and their natural habitat.

In the shimmering stream
Otter dances with delight
Graceful water sprite

Whiskers glisten bright
In the moon's soft silver light
Otter dreams take flight

Slippery slide down
River's laughter all around
Otter's joy unbound

Silent hunter waits
In the shadows of the reeds
Otter's patience yields

Mysterious eyes
Reflect the secrets of the wild
Otter's spirit thrives

These haiku poems about otters invite readers to connect with the beauty and wonder of the natural world. Through the simplicity and elegance of haiku poetry, we can appreciate the magic of otters and the delicate balance of life in the wild. Let these poems inspire you to explore the depths of nature and celebrate the creatures that make our world a more vibrant and enchanting place.

Haiku about the Tortoise

In the slow, steady
Stride of a tortoise, we find
Time's patient embrace

Shell like ancient stone
Guarding secrets of the earth
Wisdom in repose

Gentle eyes that see
Beyond the rush of the world
To moments of peace

Tortoise on the move
A wanderer of the land
Leaving trails of time

In the tortoise's gaze
We see the depth of stillness
And the beauty of grace

These haiku poems capture the essence of the tortoise, a creature that embodies the wisdom of the earth and the slow, steady pace of nature. Through their quiet presence and ancient ways, tortoises inspire us to embrace the beauty of simplicity and find peace in the rhythms of the natural world. As we reflect on these poems, may we also slow down, take time to appreciate the small wonders around us, and learn from the gentle wisdom of the tortoise.

Haiku about Penguins

Haiku, a traditional form of Japanese poetry, is the perfect way to capture the essence of the majestic and mysterious penguin. In just a few short lines, these haikus paint a vivid picture of the beauty and grace of these incredible creatures.

In the icy depths
Penguins glide with perfect grace
Black and white ballet

Waddling on the ice
Like little tuxedoed stars
Penguins steal the show

In the frozen sea
Penguins hunt for fish below
Survival dance, fierce

Nestled in the snow
Penguins huddle close for warmth
Family bond strong

Penguins march as one
Through the vast Antarctic wild
Nature's symphony

These haikus about penguins showcase the unique and captivating nature of these beloved creatures. Whether gliding through the icy waters or huddling together for warmth, penguins embody the beauty and resilience of the natural world.

Haiku about the Black Panther

In the depths of the jungle, a sleek black panther prowls, a creature of mystery and grace. Its fur glistens in the moonlight, blending seamlessly with the shadows of the night. With eyes that gleam like emeralds, it moves with a silent and deadly precision, a true predator of the wild.

Silent shadow stalks
Black panther in the moonlight
Eyes full of secrets

In the heart of the forest, the black panther reigns supreme, a symbol of power and strength. Its presence instils fear in all who cross its path, a reminder of the untamed beauty of the natural world. With every step, it leaves behind a trail of awe and wonder, a living embodiment of the wild spirit that dwells within us all

Panther in the night
Majestic, fierce and free
Nature's truest form

As the sun sets on the horizon, the black panther emerges from the shadows, a creature of the twilight hours. With a mighty roar that echoes through the trees, it announces its presence to the world, a guardian of the forest and all its inhabitants. In its eyes, one can see the ancient wisdom of the earth, a connection to a time long forgotten but never lost.

Nightfall brings the panther
A symphony of grace and power
Nature's silent king

So let us honour the black panther, a symbol of the wild and untamed beauty of the earth. In its presence, we are reminded of the delicate balance of nature, of the fierce and unyielding spirit that resides within us all. May we always remember the lessons it teaches us and strive to protect and preserve the world in which it thrives, for the black panther is a true testament to the power and wonder of the natural world.

Tawny Owl Takes to the Sky

In the stillness of the night,
Tawny owl takes to the sky,
Silent wings cutting through darkness,
A ghostly figure passing by.

Perched high in the ancient oak,
Eyes glowing with wisdom and grace,
Watching over the forest below,
A silent sentinel in this wild place.

In the moonlight, a haunting call,
Echoing through the silent air,
A voice from the depths of the woods,
A song of mystery and despair.

Tawny owl, with feathers warm,
In the cold of the winter's night,
A creature of the shadows and the stars,
A symbol of nature's eternal flight.

O' majestic owl of the night,
Your beauty and mystery inspire,
A creature of the wild and free,
In your presence, we feel the earth's fire.

The Noble Lobster

In the vast depths of the ocean,
A lobster scuttles gracefully,
Its crimson shell shining bright,
A creature of beauty and mystery.

With claws raised in defence,
It moves with a silent grace,
Navigating the rocky seabed,
A master of its watery space.

In the moonlit night,
The lobster dances a delicate dance,
Its movements fluid and precise,
A mesmerizing sight at first glance.

Oh, noble lobster,
With your ancient wisdom and strength,
You remind us of the power of nature,
And the importance of balance at great length.

So let us cherish the lobster,
In all its glory and might,
For in its presence we find,
A true marvel of the wild's delight.

Haiku about Snakes

In the depths of the forest
A serpent slithers by
Silent and swift

Coiled and waiting
Eyes like polished stones
Nature's ancient guardian

Scales shimmering
In the dappled sunlight
A creature of beauty

In its sinuous dance
A reminder of the wild
And the mysteries it holds

For poetry readers who revel in the beauty of the natural world, these haiku capture the essence of the snake - a creature both feared and revered. Through the simplicity of the haiku form, the reader is transported to the heart of the forest, where the snake moves with a quiet grace that belies its deadly nature. Each haiku paints a vivid picture of this enigmatic creature, with its shimmering scales and piercing eyes.

Haiku about Rats

In the dark corners of the world, the rat scurries unseen, a creature of the night. With its sharp eyes and twitching whiskers, it navigates the shadows with ease, a master of stealth and survival. In the urban jungle, it is often reviled as a pest, a symbol of filth and decay. But in the wild, the rat is a creature of beauty and grace, a survivor in a harsh world.

In the moonlit night,
The rat's eyes gleam like diamonds
A creature of stealth

Through the city streets
The rat moves with silent grace
A shadow in the night

In the dark forest
The rat scurries through the leaves
A whisper of life

Beneath the city
The rat finds its hidden nest
A refuge of peace

In the wild places
The rat is a survivor
A symbol of life

For those who take the time to look, the rat is a creature worth celebrating, a symbol of resilience and adaptability. In the haiku above, we see the rat in all its glory, a creature of the night, a survivor in a harsh world. Let us remember to appreciate the beauty of all creatures, no matter how small or seemingly insignificant. The rat is a reminder that life is precious, and that even the humblest of creatures has a place in this world.

Wild Rats

In the depths of the forest, where the shadows dance and the leaves whisper secrets to the wind, there lies a creature both feared and misunderstood. The wild rat, with its sleek fur and beady eyes, scurries through the undergrowth, unseen by most but ever present in the natural world. This poem is dedicated to the humble rat, a creature often overlooked but deserving of our admiration and respect.

Oh, wild rat, with your whiskers twitching and your tail held high,
You navigate the darkened paths with grace and skilful eye.
Your presence in the underbrush is both feared and reviled,
But in truth, you are a creature of the earth, wild and untamed, and should be honoured and admired.

You are a survivor, a master of adaptation,
Thriving in the harshest of environments with quiet determination.
Your cunning and intelligence are unmatched in the animal kingdom,
And though others may shun you, I see the beauty in your resilience and strength.

So, here's to the wild rat, the unsung hero of the forest,
May your kind continue to roam free and wild,
And may we learn to see the beauty in all creatures, no matter how small or misunderstood.
For in the end, we are all connected, part of the intricate web of life that binds us all together.

Majestic Eagle, A Master of the Skies

In the vast expanse of the sky, a majestic eagle soars,
With wings spread wide, it gracefully explores.
Its keen eyesight captures every detail below,
A symbol of freedom, strength, and beauty that we all know.

With feathers of gold and eyes of fire,
The eagle inspires awe and wonder, never to tire.
It rides the currents of the wind with ease,
A master of the skies, a creature to please.

In its nest high up in the mountains, it rests,
Guarding its young with love and prowess, the best.
The eagle teaches us to reach for the sky,
To spread our wings and never be shy.

So let us honour the eagle with a poem so true,
For it represents the wild, the untamed, the view.
May we all learn from its spirit so bold,
And cherish the beauty of nature, as we are told.

A Parrot's Song

In the lush rainforest, a parrot perches high,
With feathers of green and a piercing cry.
Its beak is sharp, its eyes are bright,
A creature of beauty, a colourful sight.

A parrot's song echoes through the trees,
A melody of nature, carried on the breeze.
Its words are sweet, its voice is clear,
A joyous sound for all to hear.

In flight, the parrot soars above,
A graceful dancer, a symbol of love.
Its wings spread wide, its body strong,
A creature of freedom, where it belongs.

Oh, parrot, with your vibrant hue,
You bring joy to all who gaze at you.
In the wild, you are truly free,
A symbol of nature's majesty.

So let us cherish the parrot's song,
A reminder that we all belong
To this Earth, this wondrous place,
Where creatures like the parrot grace.

Proud Peacock

In the heart of the forest, where the trees reach for the sky, there resides a magnificent creature known as the peacock. Its feathers shimmer in hues of blue, green, and gold, a sight to behold for all who are lucky enough to catch a glimpse. In this poem, we celebrate the beauty and grace of the peacock, a true marvel of the natural world.

Oh, proud peacock, with your feathers so bright,
A sight to behold in the morning light.
Your plumage gleams with colours so rare,
A true masterpiece beyond compare.

With each step you take, your feathers unfurl,
A dance of elegance that makes my heart swirl.
You strut, and you preen, a regal display,
Capturing the attention of all who pass your way.

In the stillness of the forest, you stand tall,
A symbol of beauty that enraptures us all.
Your iridescent feathers catch the sun's rays,
A dazzling spectacle that never ceases to amaze.

Oh, noble peacock, with your majestic air,
You bring a touch of magic to the world we share.
In your presence, we find a sense of wonder,
A reminder of the beauty that lies yonder.

So let us raise our voices in praise,
For the peacock's beauty that never ceases to amaze.
In this poem, we celebrate the wild and free,
And the creatures that make our world a wondrous place to be.

The Pink Flamingo

In the heart of the wetlands, where the sun sets low,
There dwells a creature with a vibrant pink glow,
With slender legs and a graceful neck that bends,
The pink flamingo stands, a beauty that transcends.

In the stillness of the water, it wades through the reeds,
A vision of elegance, fulfilling nature's needs,
Its feathers like rose petals, so delicate and light,
A sight to behold, a marvel of flight.

With every step it takes, a dance of pure grace,
In harmony with the earth, in its own special place,
A symbol of beauty, a creature so rare,
The pink flamingo, beyond compare.

So let us pause and admire this majestic bird,
A reminder of the wonders of our world,
In a world filled with chaos and strife,
The pink flamingo brings a sense of peace and life.

So, as we journey through this wild and wondrous land,
Let us not forget the beauty that nature has planned,
And let the pink flamingo's spirit soar,
In our hearts forever more.

The Melody of Birds

In the symphony of nature, the melody of bird's rings clear and sweet. Their songs fill the air with joy and wonder, echoing through the trees and across the meadows. Each species has its own unique tune, a language of love and longing that speaks to the soul of all who listen.

From the haunting call of the loon on a misty lake at dawn to the cheerful chirp of the chickadee in a snowy forest, the birdsong is a constant companion in the wilderness. Their music is a reminder of the beauty and fragility of the natural world, a testament to the power and resilience of the creatures that call it home.

The Mighty Gorilla

In the heart of the dense jungle, a majestic creature roams, swinging effortlessly from tree to tree. The mighty gorilla, with his powerful presence and gentle eyes, captivates all who are lucky enough to witness his grace. In this poem, we celebrate the beauty and strength of this incredible animal, highlighting the importance of preserving their natural habitat.

In the dappled sunlight of the forest, the gorilla stands tall, his fur gleaming in the filtered light. His movements are deliberate and purposeful, a testament to his intelligence and adaptability. As he surveys his domain, the sounds of the jungle surround him, a symphony of life that he is an integral part of. In this wild world, the gorilla reigns supreme, a symbol of the untamed beauty that we must protect.

But beneath the surface of strength and power, there is a vulnerability to the gorilla, a fragility that reminds us of our shared connection to the natural world.

Chimpanzee Swings from Vine to Vine

In the heart of the jungle, where the trees reach high,
There lives a creature with curious eyes,
The chimpanzee swings from vine to vine,
A majestic creature, so wild and so fine.

In his world of green, he dances with grace,
A symbol of freedom in his natural place,
With nimble fingers and a mischievous grin,
He moves through the forest, free from sin.

His laughter echoes through the canopy above,
A reminder of the joy found in love,
For the chimpanzee knows the secret of life,
To live in the moment, free from strife.

So, let us all learn from this wise old friend,
To cherish each moment until the very end,
For the chimpanzee teaches us to be free,
In the wild, in the heart, in the mind, let us be.

Octopus Mysterious and Unique

In the depths of the ocean, where the water is deep,
Lives a creature unlike any other, mysterious, and unique.
The octopus, with its eight arms so long and strong,
Glides through the sea, where it truly belongs.

Its body is soft, its skin can change colour,
A master of disguise, a clever underwater scholar.
It moves with grace, like a dancer in the sea,
An elegant creature, wild and free.

In the darkness of the ocean floor, it hunts for its prey,
Using its tentacles to capture, in a skilful display.
Its eyes are intelligent, full of wisdom and wonder,
A creature of the deep, a true marvel to ponder.

Oh, octopus, with your beauty and grace,
You bring a sense of awe to this watery place.
May you forever roam the ocean blue,
A symbol of wildness, strong and true.

Wild Boar, Creature of the Night

In the depths of the forest, where the shadows grow long,
There roams a creature both fierce and strong.

The wild boar, with tusks like daggers sharp,
Through the underbrush it tears apart.

Its fur, a coat of dark and matted brown,
Blending seamlessly with the earthy ground.

With a snort and a grunt, it forages for food,
Its powerful snout digging deep in the wood.

Oh, wild boar, creature of the night,
Your presence fills the forest with delight.

A symbol of strength and untamed power,
In your eyes, the fire of the wild hour.

So let us raise our voices in song,
To the wild boar, free and strong.

May we always remember the beauty you bring,
To the world of the forest, where wild creatures sing.

The Vulture Soars with Grace

In the sky, a vulture soars with grace,
A creature of beauty in a darkened place,
With wings outstretched and eyes sharp and keen,
A symbol of nature, fierce and serene.

Its feathers black against the blue,
A sight that fills the heart with awe,
As it circles high above the ground,
Searching for prey without a sound.

Its beak is sharp, its talons strong,
A hunter in the sky, where it belongs,
A scavenger of the wild and free,
A vulture in all its majesty.

Oh, vulture, with your wings unfurled,
You are a wonder of the natural world,
A symbol of life and death in one,
A creature to be admired and shunned.

So let us marvel at the vulture's flight,
And honour its place in the world's grand design,
For in its presence, we are reminded,
Of the wildness and beauty of life unconfined.

The Meerkat Dances in the Sun's Warm Embrace

In the vast and arid lands of Africa,
A creature roams with curiosity and glee,
With watchful eyes and nimble paws,
The meerkat dances in the sun's warm embrace.

Standing tall on hind legs, alert and keen,
A sentry of the desert, ever vigilant,
Their striped coats shimmering in the golden light,
A true marvel of nature's design.

In colonies they live, a tight-knit family,
Working together to survive and thrive,
Their underground burrows a network of safety,
A testament to their resilience and unity.

Oh meerkat, with your playful antics and boundless
energy,
You captivate us with your charm and grace,
A symbol of strength and adaptability,
In the wild, you find your rightful place.

So let us raise our voices in praise and awe,
For the meerkat, a creature so wild and free,
May we learn from their wisdom and tenacity,
And cherish the beauty of their existence for eternity.

The Crab Scuttles Along

In the depths of the ocean, beneath the waves,
The crab scuttles along, in its watery maze.
With claws sharp and eyes so keen,
It moves with grace, in its underwater scene.

Its shell is tough, its colours bright,
A creature of wonder, a magnificent sight.
From sandy shores to rocky caves,
The crab roams freely, in the ocean's waves.

Its movements are swift, its demeanour bold,
A true marvel of nature, a sight to behold.
In the dance of the tides, in the ebb and flow,
The crab navigates, with a rhythmic glow.

So here's to the crab, in all its glory,
A symbol of resilience, in nature's story.
May we always marvel at its beauty and grace,
In the wild world, where it finds its place.

The Cute Pot-Bellied Pig

In a quaint little farm, not too far away,
Lives a pot-bellied pig, cute as can be,
With a snout that wiggles and eyes that play,
She's a joyful creature, wild and free.

Her little trotter's patter on the ground,
As she searches for truffles, her favourite treat,
With a grunt and a squeal, a contented sound,
She waddles around, with nimble feet.

Her pink skin glistens in the morning sun,
As she rolls in the mud, without a care,
With a twinkle in her eye, she's full of fun,
This pot-bellied pig, so sweet and rare.

Oh, how I wish I could join her dance,
In the meadow, under the azure sky,
With her curly tail and a playful glance,
She's a symbol of joy, flying high.

So let us celebrate this pig so dear,
With her chubby cheeks and playful grin,
In the world of wildlife, she brings us cheer,
This pot-bellied pig, forever a win.

Pot Bellied Pigs

Pot-bellied pigs may not be the first animal that comes to mind when thinking of wildlife, but these unique creatures have a charm all their own.

With their round bodies and sweet faces, pot-bellied pigs have captured the hearts of many animal lovers around the world.

One of the most striking features of pot-bellied pigs is their distinctive appearance.

With their small, rounded bodies and short legs, they have a whimsical and endearing look that sets them apart from other animals.

Beyond their physical appearance, pot-bellied pigs also have fascinating behaviours and personalities that make them a joy to observe.

The Brown Bear

In the heart of the forest, where the trees stand tall and proud,
Lives a majestic creature, so noble and so loud.
The brown bear roams the land, with strength and grace untamed,
In the wilderness, where he is king, he cannot be restrained.

His fur is like the earth, a rich and warm shade of brown,
His eyes are deep and wise, like pools of liquid amber found.
He moves with purpose and with power, through the thick brush and trees,
A symbol of the wild, a creature of such ease.

The brown bear is a symbol of the untamed and the free,
A reminder of the beauty in the wild that we must see.
His presence is a blessing, a gift from nature's hand,
A symbol of the wild, a creature so grand.

So let us raise our voices in praise of this noble beast,
For in his strength and beauty, we find a sense of peace.
In the wild verses of the world, the brown bear stands tall and strong,
A symbol of the wild, a creature to which we belong.

The Orca Whale

In the vast expanse of the ocean blue,
A creature of beauty swims into view.
The Orca whale, with sleek black and white,
A majestic sight, a true delight.

With grace and power, it moves through the sea,
A symbol of strength and wild beauty.
Its dorsal fin cutting through the waves,
A symbol of freedom, of nature's grace.

In pods they travel, a family so tight,
Their bond unbreakable, their love so right.
Each member unique, with a role to play,
In the dance of life, in the ocean's sway.

Oh, Orca whale, so wild and free,
A symbol of nature's majesty.
We marvel at your beauty and grace,
In the vast ocean, your rightful place.

So let us celebrate this creature so grand,
In poetry and verse, let us take a stand.
To protect and preserve, for generations to come,
The Orca whale, our wild kingdom's drum.

The Scorpion

In the vast and untamed desert, where the sun beats
fiercely down,
There lies a creature of mystery, with a dangerous
reputation renowned.
The scorpion, with its venomous sting, moves stealthily
through the sand,
A fearsome predator, striking swiftly with its deadly hand.

Its armoured exoskeleton glistens in the shimmering
heat,
As it hunts for prey, with precision and speed that cannot
be beat.
Its segmented tail poised to strike, with a lethal dose of
venom to inject,
This tiny arachnid commands respect, a creature to fear
and respect.

But beyond its fearsome reputation, lies a beauty that few
can see,
In the intricacies of its design, in its resilience and
tenacity.
For the scorpion is a survivor, adapted to a harsh and
unforgiving land,
A symbol of strength and determination, a creature both
fierce and grand.

So let us marvel at the scorpion, in all its power and
grace,
A creature of the desert, with a mysterious and ancient
face.
In its silent movements, in its deadly sting,
We find a beauty and a wonder that only poetry can
bring.

The Gecko's Hunting Call

In the dim light of dusk, a tiny gecko emerges from its hiding place, its delicate feet clinging to the rough bark of a tree. Its eyes, bright and curious, dart around as it searches for its next meal. This small creature, with its intricate patterns and vibrant colours, is a marvel of nature, a true testament to the beauty and diversity of the animal kingdom.

As the gecko scampers across the branches, its movements are graceful and fluid, a dance of agility and precision. Its slender body seems to defy gravity as it effortlessly navigates its way through the dense foliage. The gecko is a master of camouflage, blending seamlessly into its surroundings with its mottled skin and intricate markings. It is a creature of stealth and cunning, a hunter in a world of predators.

In the stillness of the night, the gecko's haunting call echoes through the darkness, a haunting melody that speaks of ancient mysteries and untold secrets. Its voice is a symphony of sounds, a symphony of the wild that fills the night with its enchanting beauty. The gecko's song is a tribute to the natural world, a reminder of the interconnectedness of all living things.

As dawn breaks and the first light of morning filters through the trees, the gecko retreats to its hidden lair, its work done for another day. It is a creature of the shadows, a creature of the night, but it is also a creature of beauty and wonder. The gecko is a reminder of the magic and majesty of the natural world, a symbol of resilience and adaptability in a world of constant change.

So let us raise our voices in praise of the gecko, this tiny marvel of nature, this creature of grace and beauty. Let us celebrate its presence in our world and honour its place in the intricate web of life. For the gecko is more than just a lizard – it is a symbol of the wild, a symbol of the untamed spirit that dwells within us all.

The Lioness Roars

In the heart of the African savannah, the lioness prowls with grace and power, her golden fur shimmering in the sun. She is the queen of the jungle, fierce and fearless, a symbol of strength and beauty in the wild.

With muscles rippling beneath her sleek coat, the lioness moves with silent precision, her amber eyes scanning the horizon for prey. She is a master hunter, a predator at the top of the food chain, her every movement a testament to her supreme skill and cunning.

As she watches over her pride with fierce devotion, the lioness embodies the essence of motherhood and protection. She is a nurturing caregiver, fiercely protective of her cubs, teaching them the ways of the wild and guiding them with wisdom and love

In the stillness of the night, the lioness roars, her powerful voice echoing across the plains, a powerful reminder of her presence and dominance in the animal kingdom. Her roar is a primal call to arms, a declaration of her power and authority, a warning to all who would dare to challenge her reign.

The fierce and noble queen of the jungle, a symbol of courage and grace in the face of adversity. Let us celebrate her beauty, her strength, and her unwavering spirit, as we pay tribute to the wild and untamed beauty of the animal kingdom.

The Gorilla Reigns

In the heart of the dense jungle, a mighty gorilla roams,
With strength and power, he rules his domain,
His black fur glistens in the dappled sunlight,
A king of the wild, a majestic sight,

His eyes hold wisdom, ancient and deep,
A soul so gentle, yet fierce when he needs,
He swings through the trees with effortless grace,
A creature of beauty, in his wild, untamed space,

The gorilla's roar echoes through the trees,
A primal sound that fills the air with ease,
He is a symbol of the wild and free,
A reminder of nature's true majesty,

So let us honour this creature so grand,
With words that capture his wild, untamed land,
For in the heart of the jungle, the gorilla reigns,
A symbol of strength, in a world full of chains.

The Lemur's Playful Leaps

In the heart of the jungle, where the trees stand tall,
Lives a creature so unique, the lemurs one and all.
With wide eyes and fluffy tails, they dance and play,
In the golden sunlight, they make their way.

Their agile movements and playful leaps,
Bring joy to all who watch, their energy never sleeps.
With fur as soft as velvet and eyes so bright,
The lemurs are a breathtaking sight.

Their calls echo through the trees at night,
A symphony of nature, a beautiful sight.
They swing from branch to branch with grace,
In their forest home, they find their place.

Oh, lemurs of the wild, so free and wild,
In your world of green, you are beguiled.
May you always roam the forests fair,
For in your presence, we find peace and care.

The Wombat

In the vast and rugged wilderness of Australia, there roams a creature so unique and endearing - the wombat. These nocturnal marsupials with their stout bodies and adorable waddling gait have captured the hearts of many wildlife enthusiasts.

A wombat's burrow is a sanctuary in the earth,
Where shadows dance and whispers of the night give birth.
With sturdy claws and furry coat so soft,
In solitude, the wombat finds solace aloft.

In the moonlit darkness, it emerges to play,
With gentle grace, it roams and sniffs the way.
A creature of mystery and quiet strength,
The wombat wanders through the night's vast length.

Its round and pudgy form a sight to behold,
Innocence and wisdom in its eyes unfold.
A symbol of resilience and adaptability,
The wombat embodies nature's tranquillity.

So let us raise our voices in praise,
For the wombat's presence in the wild maze.
In its simplicity and grace, we find inspiration,
A reminder of nature's boundless fascination.

Through the power of poetry, we celebrate the wombat,
A creature of the wild, forever cherished and adored.

The Cheetah Prowls

In the vast savannah, where the sun's rays dance,
The cheetah prowls with effortless grace,
A symphony of speed and strength in every stance,
In the wild, it holds a special place.

Its coat of golden fur shimmers in the light,
As it hunts with precision, a marvel to behold,
In the blink of an eye, it takes flight,
Swift as the wind, fearless and bold.

Oh, cheetah, your beauty is unmatched,
A creature of power and elegance combined,
In your eyes, a fire that cannot be quenched,
In your presence, all other creatures resigned.

Let us marvel at the cheetah's majestic stride,
A reminder of nature's wonder and pride,
In the wild, where beauty and strength collide,
The cheetah reigns, forever wild and untied.

Swans Glide Across the Water

In the serene waters, graceful and majestic, glide the swans - symbols of beauty and elegance in the wild. Their pristine white feathers glisten in the sunlight, as they move with effortless poise and grace. The sight of these magnificent creatures is a true marvel to behold.

Their long necks curved in a perfect arc, their wings outstretched in a display of power and grace - the swans embody the essence of wild beauty.

As the swan's glide across the water, leaving ripples in their wake, they evoke a sense of tranquillity and harmony in the natural world. Their movements are fluid and graceful, a ballet of nature unfolding before our eyes.

Antelope

In the vast savannas of Africa, the graceful antelope roams free, a symbol of speed and agility in the wild. The antelope's slender legs carry it swiftly across the open plains, its eyes alert and ears perked, always on the lookout for danger. Its sleek coat shimmers in the sunlight, blending seamlessly with the golden grasses that sway in the breeze. The antelope is a symbol of freedom and grace, a reminder of the untamed beauty of the natural world.

As the antelope leaps and bounds through the wilderness, it embodies the spirit of wildness and adventure. Its movements are a dance of survival, a testament to the resilience and adaptability of nature.

The antelope's presence in the wild is a reminder of the delicate balance of nature, where predator and prey coexist in a harmonious dance of life and death.

A Rabbit Hops and Plays

In the meadow, beneath the silver moonlight,
A rabbit hops and plays, a graceful sight.
Its fur as soft as the first light of dawn,
In the wild, this creature peacefully drawn.

With ears alert, it listens for the sound,
Of predators that roam the forest ground.
But still it dances, without a care,
In its world, where magic fills the air.

Oh, rabbit of the meadow fair and bright,
Your beauty shines in the pale moonlight.
A symbol of innocence and grace,
In this wild and untamed placc.

So let us pause and admire this creature,
For its presence brings a sense of feature.
In the wild, where poetry comes alive,
The rabbit dances and thrives.

Camel

In the vast and unforgiving desert, the camel stands tall, a symbol of resilience and endurance. Its hump proudly carries the weight of survival, a testament to its ability to thrive in the harshest of environments.

The camel's eyes are deep pools of wisdom, reflecting the wisdom of centuries of survival in the harsh desert landscape. Its long lashes flutter in the hot desert breeze, a sign of its gentle nature and quiet strength.

As the camel walks across the shifting sands, its hooves leave a trail of ancient footprints, a reminder of the countless generations that have passed before it. The camel's slow and steady gait is a lesson in mindfulness and presence, a reminder to savour each moment and appreciate the beauty of the world around us.

The Puma

In the vast wilderness, where the silence speaks volumes and the shadows dance in the moonlight, there roams a creature of grace and strength - the elusive puma. With eyes like emeralds and a coat as sleek as night, the puma moves through the forest with a quiet determination, a symbol of the untamed beauty of the natural world.

In the heart of the wild, where the rivers sing and the mountains whisper secrets, the puma reigns as a queen of her domain. Her paws leave no trace as she stalks her prey, a ghost in the shadows, a predator in the night. With a fierce intelligence and a primal instinct, the puma embodies the raw power and primal essence of the wilderness.

The Chipmunk Dances

In the heart of the forest, a tiny creature scurries by,
Among the fallen leaves and branches, the chipmunk is sly,
Its stripes of brown and white, a sight to see,
A lively spirit, so wild and free,

With cheeks puffed out and nimble feet,
The chipmunk searches for food to eat,
In the quiet of the woods, it moves with grace,
A symbol of nature's beauty and pace,

Its chattering call echoes through the trees,
A playful song carried on the breeze,
The chipmunk dances in the dappled light,
A fleeting moment, a pure delight,

Oh, little chipmunk, with eyes so bright,
You bring joy and wonder to our sight,
In your world of leaves and roots,
You remind us of nature's endless pursuits,

So let us cherish the chipmunk's ways,
And honour its presence in our days,
For in its tiny form, we find,
A connection to the wild and divine.

The Ferret, Master of Stealth

In the depths of the forest, a creature so sleek,
With a coat of silver and eyes that speak,
The ferret roams, agile and sly,
A master of stealth, catching the eye.

Its slender form weaves through the brush,
A silent hunter, without a hush,
In search of prey, it prowls the night,
A ghostly figure, a shadow in flight.

With whiskers twitching, it sniffs the air,
Alert and aware, without a care,
For in the wild, the ferret reigns supreme,
A symbol of cunning, a creature of dream.

So let us admire this elusive beast,
Let its beauty be released,
For in the wild, the ferret stands tall,
A symbol of nature, a wonder for all.

In the dance of life, the ferret plays its part,
A creature of mystery, a work of art,
So let us celebrate this wondrous creature,
In the realm of poetry, let its essence feature.

The Shrew

There are creatures both large and small that captivate our hearts and minds. The shrew, a tiny, elusive mammal.

The shrew scurries through the underbrush, a blur of fur and determination. Its delicate whiskers twitch as it navigates the dense foliage, searching for insects and small invertebrates to feast upon.

Despite its diminutive size, the shrew is a fierce predator, relying on its keen senses and lightning-fast reflexes to survive in the harsh wilderness.

In the stillness of the night, the shrew emerges from its burrow, a silent shadow in the moonlit landscape. Its tiny heart beats with the rhythm of the earth, a primal pulse that connects it to the ancient forces of nature.

As the seasons change and the world transforms around it, the shrew remains steadfast in its purpose. Through the harsh winter winds and the scorching summer sun, it continues its quest for sustenance, a testament to the unyielding spirit of the wild.

The Lynx

In the heart of the forest, where the shadows dance,
There roams a creature with a stealthy advance.
The lynx cat, with eyes like emerald pools,
Moves through the trees, never leaving clues.

Its fur as soft as the evening breeze,
Its presence a mystery that never ceases.
In the moonlight, it prowls with grace,
A silent predator in a secret place.

Oh, lynx cat, with your wild soul,
You are a creature that never grows old.
Your spirit untamed, your beauty rare,
In the depths of the forest, you wander without care.

So let us raise our voices in a song,
To the lynx, so majestic and strong.
May your wild spirit forever roam free,
In the heart of the forest, where you were meant to be.

Seagulls Soar

The seagulls soar through the cerulean sky,
With graceful wings that effortlessly glide,
Their cries echo over the crashing waves,
A symphony of nature that truly amazes,

These majestic birds of the sea,
Symbolise freedom and tranquillity,
Their white feathers glistening in the sun,
As they dance and play, having so much fun,

They are the guardians of the coast,
Watching over the land they love the most,
Their presence brings a sense of calm,
A reminder of the beauty of nature's charm,

So next time you see a seagull in flight,
Take a moment to admire their grace and might,
For they are a symbol of freedom and peace,
A reminder that in nature, all troubles cease,

The seagull holds a special place,
Their beauty and grace,
So let us raise our voices in praise,
For these magnificent creatures that never cease to
amaze.

The Squid, Elusive and Free

In the deep blue sea, where mysteries abound,
A creature of wonder, the squid is found.
With tentacles long and eyes so bright,
It glides through the water, a magnificent sight.

Its body translucent, like a ghost in the night,
The squid moves gracefully, an elegant sight.
With ink as black as the deepest abyss,
It disappears into the darkness, a creature of bliss.

Oh, squid of the sea, so elusive and free,
Your beauty captivates both you and me.
In the depths of the ocean, you roam and play,
A creature of wonder, in your own special way.

So let us celebrate the squid, in all its glory,
A symbol of freedom, a part of nature's story.
For in its graceful movements, we find peace and delight,
A reminder of the beauty that surrounds us, day and night.

Canada Geese Flock

In the vast expanse of the wild, where the water meets the sky, a mesmerising sight unfolds as Canada geese flock by. Their wings beat in unison, creating a symphony of movement as they soar above the tranquil waters below. The air is filled with the sound of their honking calls, a chorus that echoes through the marshlands and fields.

As they glide gracefully through the air, the geese form intricate patterns in the sky, like a dance choreographed by nature itself. Their flight is a testament to their unity and strength as a flock, each bird playing its part in the collective journey they embark upon. It is a sight that fills the heart with wonder and awe, a reminder of the beauty and harmony that can be found in the natural world.

The geese's migration is a marvel of nature, a testament to their resilience and adaptability in the face of changing seasons and landscapes. From the frozen tundra of the Arctic to the temperate shores of the South, they travel thousands of miles in search of food and shelter. Their journey is a testament to their instinctual drive to survive and thrive in the wild.

As they land on the water with a splash, the geese create ripples that spread outwards, like a ripple effect of their presence in the world. Their presence is a reminder of the interconnectedness of all living beings, the delicate balance that exists between predator and prey, hunter and hunted. In their graceful flight and gentle calls, the geese embody the spirit of the wild, a spirit that has captivated the hearts of poets and nature lovers for centuries.

Those majestic creatures of the wild who grace our skies with their beauty and grace. Let us celebrate their resilience and strength, their unity and harmony as a flock. And let us be inspired by their example, to cherish and protect the natural world that sustains us all. For in the flight of the Canada geese, we find a reflection of our own wild spirit, a spirit that longs to be free and untamed, like the geese that flock across the skies.

Bobcat, Prince of the Night

In the vast wilderness of North America, the elusive and majestic bobcat roams freely, blending seamlessly into its surroundings with its spotted fur and piercing eyes. These solitary creatures, often mistaken for their larger cousin the mountain lion, inspire awe and admiration in those lucky enough to catch a glimpse of them in the wild.

In the stillness of the forest,
Where shadows dance and whispers linger,
There prowls a creature of grace and stealth,
The bobcat, a ghostly figure.

With eyes like golden orbs aglow,
And fur as soft as moonlight's glow,
It moves with silent, sure-footed grace,
A predator in its rightful place.

Through tangled brush and moonlit night,
The bobcat hunts with keen delight,
A symbol of the wild and free,
A creature of pure poetry.

Oh, bobcat, prince of the night,
Your presence fills us with delight,
A mystery we may never solve,
Yet in your beauty, we evolve.

So let us raise our voices high,
In praise of this wild, noble spy,
For in the bobcat's silent song,
We find our place where we belong.

For poetry lovers and wildlife enthusiasts alike, the bobcat symbolises the untamed beauty and resilience of nature. Its elusive nature and fierce independence captivate our imaginations and remind us of the inherent connection between humans and the natural world. Through the art of poetry, we can delve deeper into the mysteries of the bobcat and celebrate its place in the intricate tapestry of the wilderness.

As we reflect on the bobcat's presence in the wild, we are reminded of the delicate balance of the ecosystem and the importance of preserving these magnificent creatures for future generations to admire and cherish. Let us continue to find inspiration in the beauty of the bobcat and all creatures that inhabit the wild, using the power of poetry to amplify their voices and ensure their legacy lives on in our hearts and minds.

The Coyote

In the vast expanse of the wild, the coyote roams free, a cunning and mysterious creature that captivates the imagination of poets and nature lovers alike.

The coyote, with its sleek fur and piercing eyes, is a symbol of adaptability and resilience in the face of adversity.

The coyote is not just a symbol of beauty and grace - it is also a creature of danger and cunning.

The coyote's howl becomes a chilling reminder of the harsh realities of the natural world, where survival is a constant struggle and only the strongest and most cunning will prevail.

A creature that embodies the wild spirit of the natural world and reminds us of our own connection to the earth and all its inhabitants.

Porcupine, With Quills So Fine

Porcupines, with their quills so fine,
In the moonlight they shimmer and shine.
A creature of mystery, both feared and adored,
In the depths of the forest, they are never ignored.

Their armour of spikes, a sight to behold,
A defence mechanism, so sharp and bold.
But beneath the tough exterior lies a gentle heart,
A creature of peace, in nature's vast art.

Oh porcupine, with your quills so divine,
In the dark of the night, you truly shine.
A symbol of resilience, in a world so wild,
You teach us to be strong, yet gentle and mild.

So let us celebrate this creature so grand,
In the wild kingdom, where they stand.
For the porcupine, with its unique design,
Seeing this creature thrive, is a wonderous sign.

The Mysterious Jackal

In the heart of the desert, where the sand dunes meet the sky,
Lives a creature so elusive, with a cunning gleam in its eye.
The mysterious jackal, with its coat of silver and black,
Moves silently through the night, never leaving a track.

Its howl echoes through the darkness, haunting and surreal,
A sound that sends shivers down the spine, a feeling you can't conceal.
In the stillness of the desert, the jackal roams free,
A symbol of independence, a spirit wild and untamed, you see.

Oh, mysterious jackal, with your secrets untold,
You navigate the desert with a wisdom so old.
Your eyes hold the mysteries of the night,
A creature of darkness, a creature of light.

So, when you hear the jackal's eerie call,
Remember the beauty of the wild, the mystery of it all.
For in the heart of the desert, where the sand dunes meet the sky,
The mysterious jackal roams, a symbol of freedom, forever wild and sly.

The Jackal

In the vast and untamed wilderness, the jackal roams with stealth and grace, a creature of cunning and adaptability. In the moonlit night, its eerie howl echoes through the silent plains, a haunting melody that speaks of ancient wisdom and primal instincts.

The jackal, with its keen senses and sharp wit, is a symbol of survival and resilience in the harsh and unforgiving wilderness. Its golden eyes gleam with intelligence and cunning, a testament to its ability to thrive in the face of adversity.

Majestic Ibex

In the rugged mountains of the world, the majestic ibex
roams free,
With powerful horns that curve and twist, a sight for all to
see.
High on the cliffs they climb with ease, surefooted and
strong,
A symbol of grace and beauty, a creature that truly
belongs.

Their coats a blend of earthy tones, a perfect
camouflage,
They blend in with the rocky terrain, like a perfectly
scripted montage.
Their eyes are keen, their senses sharp, always on alert,
Surviving in the harsh wilderness, where only the fittest
can assert.

So let us enjoy this noble beast,
For the ibex that roams the mountains, its spirit never
ceased.
In the realm of animal poetry, let its name be known,
A symbol of strength and beauty, in the wild kingdom it
has grown.

The Antelope Leaps

In the vast savannas where the sun shines bright,
The antelope leaps with grace and might.
Its slender legs carry it across the land,
A symbol of freedom, wild and grand.

With eyes that sparkle like the stars above,
The antelope embodies beauty and love.
Its coat, a tapestry of earthy tones,
Blending seamlessly with the grassy zones.

In the stillness of the morning air,
The antelope moves without a care.
Its spirit untamed, its heart so pure,
A creature of the wild, forever sure.

Oh, antelope, with your spirit free,
You inspire us with your grace and beauty.
May we learn from you to live in harmony,
With nature and all its wonders, for eternity.

The Moose, Truly Wild and Free

In the vast and untamed wilderness,
Roams the majestic moose, so grand,
With antlers reaching towards the sky,
A symbol of strength and grace,

In the stillness of the forest,
The moose moves with such ease,
A silent giant among the trees,
A sight to behold, a creature of peace,

Its coat as dark as night,
Its eyes so deep and wise,
The moose embodies the spirit,
Of the wild, untamed, and free,

So let us raise our voices,
In praise of this noble beast,
For in its presence we are reminded,
Of the beauty of nature's feast,

May the moose forever roam,
In the forests and the streams,
A symbol of the wild and free,
A creature of our dreams.

Frogs Croak

In the tranquil marshlands where lilies bloom,
The chorus of croaking frogs fills the room.
Their symphony of sounds, both loud and clear,
Echoes through the night, bringing joy near.

With skin as smooth as the water they dwell,
Frogs leap and play with a graceful spell.
Their vibrant colours, a sight to behold,
In shades of green and gold, so bold.

Oh, how they hop and leap with glee,
In the cool waters, wild and free.
Their eyes shining bright in the moonlit night,
Guiding them through the darkness with delight.

So let us celebrate these creatures of the pond,
In their watery world, they are so fond.
With their playful antics and joyful song,
Frogs remind us to dance and sing along.

The Noble Camel

In the vast, sandy deserts of the world, the majestic camel roams with grace and pride. Its hump sways with each step, a symbol of resilience and strength in the harsh wilderness.

With a steady gait and a solemn stare,
The camel crosses the desert with flair.
Its long, slender legs carry it with ease,
Through the scorching heat and shifting breeze.

Oh, noble camel, with your hump so high,
You are a symbol of endurance under the sky.
Your eyes, deep and wise, hold ancient secrets,
Of journeys taken through deserts and regrets.

In your heart lies a quiet strength,
A resilience that knows no length.
You trek through the sands with poise and grace,
A creature of beauty in a desolate place.

So let us raise our voices in praise,
For the camel, with its regal gaze.
We celebrate your resilience and charm,
Oh, noble creature of the desert, so calm.

The Hippo

In the vast savannahs where the river flows,
Lives a creature gentle yet mighty, the hippo.
With a massive body and a wide, toothy grin,
This herbivorous giant is a sight to behold within.

His skin as tough as armour, a shade of muddy brown,
He lumbers through the water, never making a sound.
But don't be fooled by his peaceful demeanour,
For when threatened, he can charge with a force that's extreme.

In the depths of the river, he finds his true home,
Among the lilies and reeds, where he loves to roam.
With eyes that sparkle like the stars in the sky,
The hippo is a symbol of power and grace, so sly.

So let us raise our voices in praise of this beast,
Whose presence in the wild is a true feast.
For in his gentle gaze, we find a connection,
To the wonders of nature, a divine reflection.

The Raccoon, Silent and Shy

In the dead of night, the raccoon creeps,
Silent and sly, with eyes that gleam,
A masked bandit of the moonlit streets,
Stealing away on nimble feet.

With dexterous paws and a clever mind,
The raccoon searches for treasures to find,
In the trash bins and under the stars,
This clever creature leaves no bars.

Oh, raccoon with your mischievous ways,
You navigate the urban maze,
Surviving on scraps and stolen delights,
A creature of the shadowed nights.

But in your cunning and your grace,
There is a beauty in your wild embrace,
A reminder of the untamed world,
Where nature's wonders are unfurled.

So let us raise a toast to thee,
O noble raccoon, wild and free,
For in your antics and your charm,
You remind us of nature's endless charm.

Kangaroo and Her Joey

In the vast and untamed land of Australia,
Roams a creature both unique and wild,
The kangaroo with her joey by her side,
In perfect harmony, mother, and child.

With grace and agility, they hop and play,
Their bond unbreakable, come what may,
The joey snug in his mother's pouch,
Protected and loved, they always crouch.

In the land down under, where the sun shines bright,
The kangaroo and her joey take flight,
Bounding across the red earth with ease,
A sight to behold, a true masterpiece.

Their love knows no bounds, their loyalty true,
In the vast outback, they stick like glue,
So here's to the kangaroo and her joey,
A pair so special, so full of joy and glee.

Birds of Prey

In the vast expanse of the sky, with wings spread wide,
The birds of prey soar, majestic and dignified.
Their keen eyesight pierces through the darkness of
night,
Hunting their prey with stealth and might.

The eagle, with its regal presence and powerful beak,
Symbolises freedom, courage, at its peak.
It soars above the mountains, a creature of grace,
A symbol of strength in every place.

The hawk, with its sharp talons and piercing cry,
Is a hunter in the sky, swift and sly.
Its wingspan wide, its flight precise,
It is a marvel of nature, a creature of ice.

The falcon, with its incredible speed and agility,
Dives and swoops with unparalleled ability.
Its keen sense of sight and deadly precision,
Make it a fearsome predator in its mission.

In the realm of the wild, where only the strong survive,
The birds of prey reign supreme, keeping nature alive.
Their beauty and power captivate the eye,
In the wild kingdom, they truly fly high.

Colourful Parrots

In the vibrant world of the animal kingdom, few creatures capture the imagination quite like the colourful parrots. Their dazzling plumage and lively personalities make them a favourite subject for poets and artists alike.

Behold the parrots, with feathers bright,
Their colours a dazzling, wondrous sight.
From emerald, green to sapphire blue,
Their rainbow hues delight the view.
With a flash of red and a splash of gold,
These feathered gems never grow old.

In the jungle's canopy they soar,
Their voices ringing out, a joyful roar.
Their laughter fills the air with glee,
A symphony of sound, wild and free.
Oh, how we envy their carefree ways,
As they dance among the sunlit rays.

Each parrot is a work of art,
A masterpiece created with love and heart.
Their wings spread wide, they take to flight,
A breathtaking display of pure delight.
In their world of colour and song,
We find a place where we truly belong.

So let us raise a toast to the parrots bold,
Whose beauty and grace will never grow old.
May their colours brighten our darkest days,
And their songs inspire us in countless ways.
For in the poetry of their vibrant wings,
We find a world where beauty truly sings.

Mysterious Sea Creatures

In the depths of the ocean, where sunlight cannot reach,
There dwell mysterious creatures, strange and unique.
With glowing eyes and scales that shimmer in the dark,
These sea creatures roam, leaving their mark.

A poem about the mysterious beings of the sea,
Is sure to captivate poetry lovers like you and me.
From the elusive anglerfish with its dangling lure,
To the graceful jellyfish, drifting without a care.

The octopus with its eight arms, dancing in the tide,
And the giant squid, lurking deep and wide.
Each creature holds a secret, a story untold,
Waiting to be discovered, in the depths so cold.

So let us dive into the world of the unknown,
And explore the mysteries of the ocean's throne.
For in the depths of the sea, where the light does not reach,
Lies a world of wonder, waiting for us to teach.

Elegant Dolphin's

In the vast expanse of the ocean blue,
Dolphin's dance and play, a graceful crew.
Their sleek bodies glide through the waves,
Elegant creatures, the sea their domain's raves.

With a flick of their tail, they leap and spin,
Their movements fluid, a mesmerizing din.
Their clicks and whistles fill the air,
A language of love, joy, and care.

In pods they swim, a family tight knit,
Their bond unbreakable, a beautiful fit.
They communicate with a sense of grace,
Their intelligence a marvel, a wonder to embrace.

Oh, elegant dolphins, so free and wild,
In your world of water, you are beguiled.
We watch in awe, inspired by your beauty,
In poems and verses, we honour your duty.

So let us raise our voices high,
And sing of dolphins in the sky.
For in their presence, we find solace,
In their elegance, we find grace.

Piranha

In the depths of the Amazon River, where the waters run deep and dark, lurks a creature feared by all - the mighty piranha. With razor-sharp teeth and a voracious appetite, this fish strikes fear into the hearts of those who dare to enter its domain. But beneath its fearsome exterior lies a creature of beauty and grace, as this poem about the piranha will reveal.

Oh piranha, fierce and swift,
In the river's depths you drift,
Your jaws like daggers, sharp and keen,
A predator, feared and unseen.

Beneath the surface, you await,
For unsuspecting prey to take the bait,
Your hunger never satisfied,
In the shadows, you reside.

But in your sleek and silvery form,
There lies a beauty, wild and warm,
A creature of the waters deep,
Guardian of secrets that we keep.

So let us not judge you by your bite,
But see the beauty in your might,
For in the wild, you have your place,
A symbol of the river's grace.

Sea Urchin, with Spines so Sharp

In the depth of the ocean blue,
Lies a creature unique and true,
The sea urchin, with spines so sharp,
Yet harbouring beauty in its heart.

Its form a marvel of symmetry,
A globe of spikes, a sight to see,
In colours ranging from bright to bold,
A masterpiece of nature, one to behold,

Beneath the waves it quietly roams,
A gentle creature in its home,
Feeding on algae, drifting by,
A peaceful presence, under the sky.

Oh, sea urchin, with your spiny grace,
A wonder of the ocean's embrace,
In your quiet world, you do thrive,
A testament to life's will to survive.

So let us marvel at this creature small,
A poem for the sea urchin, standing tall,
In the vast expanse of the ocean's blue,
A reminder of nature's wonders, ever true.

Hammerhead Shark, with Eyes that Gleam

In the deep blue sea, where shadows dance,
A creature prowls with a deadly stance,
The hammerhead shark, with eyes that gleam
In the moonlit waters, a fearsome dream,

Its head shaped like a hammer, strong and true,
A predator of the ocean, in search of its due,
With razor-sharp teeth and a powerful bite,
It rules the waters with all its might,

Swimming silently through the waves,
The hammerhead stalks its prey, never slaves,
To the whims of the currents, it hunts with precision,
A master of stealth, a creature on a mission,

So let us marvel at this majestic beast,
A symbol of power, a symbol of the east,
In the vast expanse of the ocean's domain,
The hammerhead shark shall forever reign.

The Mighty Hippopotamus

In the vast savannahs of Africa, the mighty hippopotamus roams,
A creature of immense strength and grace, but its future is unknown.
Once revered by ancient civilizations, now threatened by man's greed,
This poem tells the tale of the plight of the hippo, a creature in need.

With its massive frame and powerful jaws, the hippo is a force to be reckoned,
But its habitat is disappearing, its numbers steadily beckoned.
Poachers hunt them for their ivory tusks, their meat, and their hides,
Leaving these majestic animals fighting for survival on all sides.

In the rivers and lakes where they once thrived, pollution now runs deep,
Chemicals and waste poisoning their homes, a nightmare they cannot sleep.
Their once tranquil waters now tainted with toxins, their food sources deplete,
The hippopotamus struggles to find a safe haven, a place where it can retreat.

The Puma, Creature of Grace

In the heart of the forest, where shadows dance,
Lies a creature of grace, in a swift, silent trance.
The puma, sleek and strong, with eyes of gold,
Roams the wilds, a predator bold.

With sinewy muscles and a coat of fur,
The puma moves with a quiet, deadly allure.
Through the trees it stalks, a ghost in the night,
A symbol of power, of strength and of might.

Its golden eyes gleam in the moon's soft glow,
A hunter supreme, with a deadly blow.
For the puma is a creature of the wild,
A symbol of freedom, fierce and untamed, undefiled.

So let us raise our voices in a song of praise,
For the puma, the guardian of the forest's maze.
May it forever roam the wild lands free,
A majestic creature, for all to see.

In the heart of the forest, where shadows dance,
Lies a creature of grace, in a swift, silent trance.
The puma, a symbol of power and grace,
In the wilds of nature, finds its rightful place.

The Black Panther

In the depths of the dense jungle, the Black Panther prowls,
Its sleek ebony coat glistening in the moon's soft light.
With eyes like glowing embers and muscles coiled tight,
This majestic creature moves with silent grace, its presence howls.

A symbol of strength and power, the Black Panther reigns,
A predator unmatched, a master of the night.
Its stealth and cunning make it a fearsome sight,
A creature of legend that forever remains.

In the heart of Africa, the Black Panther roams,
A living shadow, a ghost of the night.
Its beauty and mystery fill us with awe and delight,
A creature of darkness, a creature of ancient tomes.

So let us raise our voices in praise of this majestic beast,
Let us honour its beauty, its grace, and its sheer power.
For the Black Panther is a symbol, a creature untamed,
A reminder of the wildness that lies within us, the beauty we seek.

The Crafty Coyote

In the vast expanse of the wild, there roams a creature with cunning eyes and a sly grin. Crafty Coyote, the master of deception, moves through the shadows with grace and stealth. This poem delves into the enigmatic nature of this elusive predator, capturing the essence of its wild spirit.

Crafty Coyote, with your silver fur,
You prowl the night with silent purr.
Your eyes gleam with mischief and glee,
A trickster of the highest degree.

In the moonlit night, you dance and play,
Your howls echoing in the dark, far away.
You are the embodiment of the wild,
A creature of mystery, untamed and beguiled.

Crafty Coyote, with your clever ways,
You navigate the world with a knowing gaze.
You outsmart your foes with cunning schemes,
A master of survival, in the realm of dreams.

In the realm of nature, you reign supreme,
A symbol of adaptability, in the grand scheme.
Crafty Coyote, we marvel at your guile,
A creature of the wild, forever agile.

Salamanders

Deep in the forest, where the shadows dance,
There lies a creature with a fiery glance.
The salamander, sleek and sly,
Moves through the undergrowth with a silent sigh.

Its skin shines like polished brass,
A rainbow of colours as it slithers past.
With eyes like jewels, it surveys its domain,
A master of stealth, a creature untamed.

In the cool of the night, it emerges from its lair,
A creature of magic, of mystery and flair.
With a flick of its tail, it disappears from sight,
Leaving behind only whispers of its midnight flight.

Oh, salamander, creature of the wild,
In your presence, we are beguiled.
Your beauty and grace, a sight to behold,
A reminder of nature's wonders untold.

So let us raise our voices in praise,
For the salamander, in all its maze.
A creature of wonder, of beauty and grace,
A symbol of nature's eternal embrace.

Slithering Snakes

In the forests and jungles, where shadows dance,
The slithering snakes silently advance.
Their scales glisten in the moonlight's glow,
As they move with grace, both fast and slow.

Their tongues flicker in and out,
Detecting scents without a doubt.
They glide through the grass with ease,
A sight that can make a person freeze.

Some fear them for their venomous bite,
But others see them as a symbol of might.
For snakes are creatures of the wild,
Their presence leaving us beguiled.

So let us admire these creatures so sleek,
As they move through the world, silent and meek.
For in their slithering dance, we can find,
A beauty that is truly one of a kind.

Regal Turtles

In the vast world of wildlife, there are creatures that captivate our imagination with their majestic presence. One such creature is the regal turtle, a symbol of wisdom, longevity, and resilience. These ancient reptiles have roamed the earth for millions of years, embodying a sense of timelessness and grace.

In the realm of poetry inspired by nature's creatures, the regal turtle holds a special place. Its slow and deliberate movements, its shell adorned with intricate patterns, and its wise gaze all serve as sources of inspiration for poets seeking to capture the essence of this magnificent creature.

In the quiet waters of ponds and lakes, the regal turtle moves with quiet grace, its ancient wisdom shining through its eyes. The turtle's shell becomes a metaphor for protection and resilience, a symbol of the ability to weather life's storms with grace and dignity.

The regal turtle becomes a symbol of the interconnectedness of all living beings, a reminder of the beauty and wonder that surrounds us in the wild.

In the vast tapestry of nature's creatures, the regal turtle stands out as a symbol of wisdom, resilience, and grace.

The Croaking of Frogs

In the still of the night, a chorus begins to rise,
The croaking of frogs, a symphony in disguise.
Their voices blend together, creating a melodious tune,
A song of the wild, under the light of the moon.

The marsh comes alive with their vibrant calls,
Echoing through the trees, bouncing off the walls.
Each croak is a message, a call to their mates,
A love song in the darkness, sealing their fates.

Their serenade is haunting, a sound so pure,
A reminder of nature's beauty, strong and sure.
Their croaking is a language, one we may never
understand,
But we can appreciate its beauty, across the land.

So next time you hear the frogs singing in the night,
Take a moment to listen, let their music take flight.
For in their croaks lies a story, a tale of the wild,
A poem of nature, sung by each croaking child.

Vibrant Poison Dart Frogs

In the heart of the rainforest, where colours dance and nature sings, resides the vibrant poison dart frog. Its tiny body adorned with hues of electric blue, fiery red, and shimmering gold. This tiny creature, no larger than a thumbnail, is a marvel of nature's design. Its poison, a deadly defence against predators, is a reminder of the delicate balance of life in the wild.

In the depths of the jungle, where shadows play and sunlight filters through the canopy, the poison dart frog moves with grace and agility. Its movements are like poetry in motion, a delicate dance that captivates the eye and stirs the soul. Each leap, each twist, each turn is a testament to the frog's resilience and strength in the face of danger.

In the silence of the forest, where only the rustle of leaves and the chirping of insects can be heard, the poison dart frog calls out to its mate. Its song is a symphony of love and longing, a melody that echoes through the trees and reverberates in the hearts of all who hear it. It is a reminder of the power of connection and the beauty of relationships in the natural world.

Mysterious Bats

In the dead of night, when the moon hangs high,
Mysterious bats take to the sky.
Their wings like shadows, silent and sleek,
They glide through the darkness, swift and meek.

In caves and forests, they make their home,
Their echolocation guides them as they roam.
Their eyes see what others cannot,
Invisible to the naked eye, their secrets are sought.

Oh, how they dance in the midnight air,
Their fluttering forms beyond compare.
Like phantoms they move with grace,
A sight that time cannot erase.

So let us marvel at these creatures of the night,
Their beauty and mystery shining bright.
For in the darkness, they find their way,
Guided by instinct, they never stray.

Creeping Spiders

In the shadows of the night,
Where darkness meets the light,
Creeping spiders weave their webs,
Silent hunters, with delicate threads.

Their eight legs move with grace,
As they search for prey to chase,
In the corners of our homes,
Or in the wilderness where they roam.

With eyes that see in the dark,
And fangs that leave a mark,
Spiders are nature's architects,
Creating masterpieces with intricate specs.

So next time you see a spider,
Don't be quick to squish or deride her,
For she is a creature of wonder,
A spinner of silk, a silent hunter.

Let us admire these creatures small,
For they are a vital part of nature's call,
In the web of life, they play their part,
A symbol of beauty, in every heart.

So let us appreciate these creeping spiders,
For they are truly nature's insiders,
In the wild, they silently reside,
A reminder of the beauty in every stride.

Bushbabies Leap

In the dark of night,
Bushbabies leap from tree to tree,
Silent and swift,
Their eyes glowing with curiosity.

Ears like satellite dishes,
Twitching at every sound,
They dance among the branches,
In the moonlight they are found.

Tiny hands reach out,
Grasping for a tasty treat,
Bushbabies are the acrobats of the night,
Their movements so light and fleet.

In the heart of the jungle,
Bushbabies sing their sweet song,
A symphony of chirps and trills,
Nature's creatures, wild and strong.

So let us pause and listen,
To the bushbabies' whispered call,
For in their song we find
The beauty of nature, standing tall.

Haiku about Porpoise

In the deep blue sea
Porpoise dances with the waves
Graceful and joyful

Sleek and swift they glide
Through the ocean's vast expanse
Majestic beings

Their playful nature
Brings smiles to all who see them
Pure joy in motion

Porpoise, gentle souls
Protectors of the ocean
We must cherish them

Let us learn from them
To live in harmony with
Nature's wonders free

Haiku about Rabbits

In the meadow's edge
Ears twitching in the moonlight
Silent shadows hop

Soft fur in the breeze
Nose twitching eyes bright with glee
Nature's gentle grace

Whiskers in the grass
Bounding through the fields with joy
Rabbits dance in light

Furry friends of mine
Hopping through the wilds so free
Nature's poetry

In the quiet woods
Rabbits play in golden sun
Nature's harmony

Haiku about Hedgehogs

In the moonlit night
Hedgehog scurries unseen
Nature's tiny ghost

Prickly ball of spikes
Curling up in self-defence
Hidden from the world

Underneath the brush
Hedgehog roams in secret
Nature's quiet spy

Soft snuffling noises
Echo through the silent woods
Hedgehog on the hunt

In the early dawn
Hedgehog bids farewell to night
Nature's gentle friend

For poetry readers who appreciate the beauty of wildlife, hedgehogs are a fascinating subject to explore through the ancient art of haiku. These short, three-line poems capture the essence of these elusive creatures as they navigate their nocturnal world. The imagery of a hedgehog as a "prickly ball of spikes" or a "nature's tiny ghost" evokes a sense of mystery and wonder that is sure to resonate with lovers of wildlife poetry.

Hedgehogs are often misunderstood creatures, known for their defensive posture of curling up into a ball of spikes when threatened. This behaviour is beautifully captured in haiku form, highlighting the delicate balance between vulnerability and resilience that hedgehogs exhibit in the wild. As they scurry through the moonlit night or roam in secret under the brush, hedgehogs become nature's quiet spies, observing the world around them.

Haiku about Snails

Slowly they crawl by
Tiny shells glistening bright
Snails in moon's soft light

Trails of silver slime
Left behind on forest floor
Nature's artwork shines

In gardens they roam
Seeking out tender green leaves
Nature's gentle pests

Ancient wisdom held
In their spiral-shaped abode
Secrets left untold

Oh, tiny snails dear
In your world of slow motion
Peace and beauty near

We hope these haikus have allowed you to appreciate
the quiet grace and charm of snails in a new light. May
their slow and steady presence inspire you to slow down
and appreciate the simple wonders of the natural world
around us.

Haiku about Peacocks

Peacocks are majestic creatures that captivate us with their vibrant feathers and graceful movements. In this subchapter, we explore the beauty of peacocks through the art of haiku, a form of Japanese poetry that captures the essence of a moment in just a few simple lines.

Feathers unfurl wide
A rainbow in the sunlight
Peacock's dance of pride

Eyes like ancient stars
Peacock guards its hidden truths
Silent, wise, and still

Peacock in the woods
Echoes of the forest's song
A creature of grace

Feathers fade to grey
Peacock's dance comes to an end
Silent in the dusk

Haiku about Falcon

In the sky he soars
Wings outstretched with eyes so keen
Falcon hunts below

Swift predator's flight
Silent shadow in the sky
Nature's perfect hunt

Feathers sleek and strong
Falcon dives, strikes with purpose
Wildlife's noble king

Majestic bird of prey
Falcon's beauty takes my breath
Nature's fierce beauty

In the wild he roams
Falcon's spirit wild and free
Soaring high

These haikus capture the essence of the falcon, a
creature of grace and power in the natural world. For
poetry readers who appreciate the beauty of wildlife
poetry, these verses offer a glimpse into the world of this
magnificent bird. The imagery of the falcon's flight,
hunting prowess, and regal presence is sure to resonate
with those who find inspiration in the wonders of the
animal kingdom.

Alligator Bites

An alligator bites;
With a grip so tight,

A feeding frenzy, is usually its plight,
Tugging and pulling, with all its might,

It truly puts up, one hell of a fight,
Reaching up out of the water, to some height,

If you ever witness this, it will give you a fright,
Something to behold, and quite a sight.

Meerkats

In the vast expanse of the African plains,
Lives a creature that never complains.
With their sleek bodies and curious eyes,
Meerkats are a sight that truly mesmerize.

They live in close-knit families, called a mob,
Working together, they search for food to gob.
Their burrows are intricate, with tunnels that twist,
A safe haven for rest, where they can coexist.

Meerkats are always on the lookout,
For predators that might lurk about.
Their sentinels stand tall and alert,
Ensuring the safety of their desert turf.

In the golden light of the setting sun,
Meerkats frolic and play, having fun.
Their antics bring joy to all who see,
A symbol of wild and carefree glee.

So let us raise a toast to these creatures so dear,
Meerkats, the guardians of the African frontier.
In their unity and strength, we find inspiration,
A testament to the power of cooperation.

The Tasmanian Devil

The Tasmanian Devil, a creature of the night,
With sharp teeth and a fierce appetite,
Roaming the Australian wilderness,
A sight to behold, one to impress.

Its fur is black as the darkest night,
Its eyes gleam with a fiery light,
A symbol of power and strength,
In the wild, it goes to great lengths.

Its growl is fearsome, its snarl a warning,
To those who dare to cross its path in the morning,
But beneath that tough exterior,
Lies a creature with a heart so superior.

For the Tasmanian Devil is not all brute force,
It's a survivor, a creature of resource,
In a world where only the strong survive,
The Tasmanian Devil thrives.

So let us admire this creature of the wild,
For in its presence, we are beguiled,
By its beauty, its strength, its grace,
The Tasmanian Devil, a creature we must embrace.

Oh, Little Mouse

In the dark corners of the world, where shadows dance
and moonlight gleams,
There lies a tiny creature, with eyes as bright as
moonbeams.
The mouse, so small and fragile, scurrying through the
night,
In search of crumbs and shelter, always ready for a fight.

With whiskers twitching, ears alert, they navigate their
way,
Through fields and forests, barns, and homes, where
they quietly stay.
Their tails a slender ribbon, their fur a soft grey hue,
Mice are the unsung heroes, of the wilderness they
knew.

They may be small in stature, but their hearts are brave
and true,
Facing dangers every day, yet always persevering
through.
So let us raise our voices, in praise of these creatures so
dear,
For in their tiny hearts, a wild spirit we can hear.

Oh, little mouse, so swift and sly, we honour you this day,
For in your humble presence, we find a sense of play.
In fields and forests, barns, and homes, you quietly
reside,
A symbol of resilience, in the wild world outside.

Reindeer Roam

In the frosty winter air, the reindeer roam,
Their hooves pounding on the frozen ground,
Majestic creatures of the Arctic zone,
Their beauty and grace truly astound,

With antlers raised towards the sky,
They prance and play in the snow,
Their coats a shimmering hue of silver and white,
A sight that fills the heart with awe,

In the silence of the wilderness they stand,
A symbol of strength and endurance,
Surviving in a harsh and unforgiving land,
Their resilience is truly a marvel to witness,

So let us raise our voices in praise,
For these noble creatures of the north,
In their presence, we find solace and peace,
A reminder of the beauty of the earth's wild worth.

Haiku about The Anteater

In the dark of night
Anteater prowls for its prey
Silent, deadly grace

Long snout sniffs the air
Seeking out termite morsels
Nature's vacuum cleaner

Striped coat gleams in moonlight
A creature of stealth and skill
Master of disguise

Giant claws dig deep
Into earth, where ants reside
Anteater feasts well

Majestic creature
Symbol of patience and strength
Anteater roams free

For poetry readers who have a love for wildlife, the haiku about the anteater captures the essence of this fascinating creature. With its long snout and giant claws, the anteater is a symbol of patience and strength in the animal kingdom. As it prowls for its prey in the dark of night, the anteater displays silent, deadly grace that is both captivating and awe-inspiring. Its striped coat gleams in the moonlight, making it a master of disguise in the wild.

The haiku paints a vivid picture of the anteater as a creature of stealth and skill, seeking out termite morsels with precision and determination. With its giant claws digging deep into the earth, the anteater feasts well on ants, showcasing its mastery over its natural environment. This majestic creature serves as a reminder of the beauty and complexity of the wildlife that surrounds us, and the importance of preserving their habitats for future generations to enjoy.

Haiku about The Tasmanian Devil

In the shadows lurks
The Tasmanian devil
Fierce and wild at heart

Black fur and red eyes
A creature of mystery
Roaming the night skies

Sharp teeth, powerful jaws
Ready to pounce and attack
A fearsome predator

In the darkness deep
The devil's haunting cry echoes
A wild symphony

Respect the devil
For it is part of nature
A true force of wild

Crows Caw with Haunting Cries

In the deep forests and open skies, the crows soar and caw with haunting cries. Their black feathers glisten in the sun, as they dance and play, having so much fun. A symbol of mystery and wisdom, these birds captivate our hearts and minds, leaving us in awe of their beauty and grace.

In the still of the night, the crows gather in trees, their dark silhouettes against the moonlit breeze. They chatter and caw, their voices echoing through the night, a chorus of sound that fills us with delight. These creatures of the night, with eyes so bright, tell stories of old and secrets untold.

With their keen intelligence and sharp wit, the crows navigate the world with ease and grit. They are scavengers and survivors, adapting to any environment with cunning and guile. With their playful antics and mischievous ways, the crows remind us of the wildness that still resides within us all.

In ancient lore and myth, the crow is a symbol of death and rebirth, a messenger between the worlds of the living and the dead. They are omens of change and transformation, guiding us through the darkness with their wisdom and insight. The crows are guardians of the wild, protectors of the earth.

So let us raise our voices in praise of the crows, these mysterious creatures with hearts of gold. Let us honour their presence in our world and celebrate the beauty and wonder they bring. For in the call of the wild, we find our true selves reflected in the eyes of the crows, forever free and wild.

The Eagle Owl

In the vast wilderness of the night,
The Eagle Owl takes to flight,
With wings outstretched, it soars above,
A symbol of wisdom, strength, and love.

Its piercing eyes, a sight to behold,
Gleaming like diamonds, shining bold,
In the darkness, it hunts with grace,
A silent predator in its rightful place.

Majestic creature of the night,
Guided by the moon's soft light,
It calls out with a haunting cry,
A song that echoes through the sky.

Oh, Eagle Owl, so grand and wise,
Your presence fills the darkened skies,
A symbol of the wild and free,
A reminder of what we could be.

So let us learn from this noble bird,
To embrace the wild, let our voices be heard,
For in the heart of nature, we find our true selves,
In the call of the wild, where the Eagle Owl dwells.

Haiku about Love Birds

In the treetops high
Love birds sing their sweet duet
A melody of joy

Feathers of vibrant hue
Entwined in graceful dance
Two hearts beat as one

Nestled in their home
A sanctuary of love
Whispers in the wind

Morning light reveals
Love birds in tender embrace
A bond that never fades

Through storm and through calm
Love birds soar through life as one
Infinite love's song

Haiku about Barn Owls

In the moonlit night
Silent wings swoop down to hunt
Barn owl's ghostly flight

Feathers soft and white
Eyes like glowing amber gems
Majestic and wise

Perched in ancient barns
Guardians of the night sky
Whispering secrets

Hunting without sound
Silent death in velvet wings
Nature's perfect ghost

Barn owl, spirit bird
Mysterious and graceful
Wild beauty untamed

For poetry readers who appreciate the beauty of wildlife, these haiku capture the essence of the majestic barn owl. With its silent flight and piercing gaze, the barn owl is a symbol of mystery and wisdom in the night. Its presence in ancient barns adds to its allure, as it watches over the land with a quiet intensity. Through these haiku, we are reminded of the delicate balance of nature and the untamed beauty of the wild. In the world of wildlife poetry, the barn owl stands as a symbol of the unseen mysteries of the natural world.

Firefly Glowing

In the serene darkness of the night,
A tiny firefly begins to ignite,
Its soft glow flickering in the air,
Guiding lost souls with a gentle flair.

Like a beacon in the night,
The firefly's glow shines so bright,
A symbol of hope in the wild,
A reminder of nature's beauty, undefiled.

In the dance of the firefly's light,
We find solace in the midst of night,
A miniature star, a spark of life,
Amidst the chaos and strife.

Oh firefly, glowing so bright,
In the cloak of darkness, a guiding light,
Your presence brings peace and calm,
In the wildest of nature's balm.

So let us cherish the firefly's glow,
A symbol of beauty in nature's show,
In the call of the wild, we find solace,
In the firefly's gentle embrace.

Haiku about Firefly

Haiku, a traditional form of Japanese poetry, is perfect for capturing the fleeting beauty of a firefly. These tiny creatures, with their glowing bodies, have captivated poets and nature lovers for centuries. In just a few short lines, a haiku can convey the magic and wonder of a firefly's dance in the night.

Glowing in the dark
A firefly's light beckons me
To follow its path

In the still of the night
The firefly's dance begins
A flickering spark

A tiny lantern
Guiding me through the darkness
Firefly's gentle glow

In the summer air
Fireflies twinkle like stars
Nature's own light show

Oh firefly, so bright
Your light brings joy to my soul
In the dark of night

These haiku capture the essence of the firefly, a creature that symbolises the beauty and mystery of the natural world. Whether you're a seasoned poetry reader or new to the world of animal poetry, these verses are sure to inspire and delight. Take a moment to appreciate the simple magic of a firefly's light, and let these haiku transport you to a world of wonder and enchantment.

Oh Aardvark

In the vast savannahs of Africa, the aardvark roams,
With its long snout and sturdy claws, it seeks out termite homes.
A creature of the night, it digs with skill and grace,
Feasting on insects in the dark, a silent hunter in its place.

Oh aardvark, mysterious creature of the night,
With your earthy scent and gentle eyes so bright.
You move through the shadows with a quiet grace,
A symbol of resilience in this wild and untamed place.

Your coat of armour protects you from harm,
As you navigate the darkness with calm and charm.
A symbol of perseverance, in a world so harsh,
You inspire us to keep going, even when life seems dark.

So let us raise our voices in praise of the aardvark,
A creature of the night, a symbol of the wild and stark.
In your quiet ways, you teach us to endure,
To face our struggles with strength and to never be demure.

Oh aardvark, a creature calm and wise,
In your presence, we see the beauty in the wild's disguise.
May we learn from you, in our own journey through the dark,
And find the strength to carry on, like the resilient aardvark.

Stick Insects

In the quiet shadows of the forest, where the leaves rustle gently in the wind, there resides a creature so unique and fascinating - the stick insects. These remarkable insects blend seamlessly with the branches and twigs, their slender bodies mimicking the very essence of nature itself. It is as though they are a part of the trees, an extension of the earth's beauty.

In their delicate movements and graceful sways, the stick insects tell a story of patience and resilience. They teach us the art of camouflage, the ability to adapt and survive in a world that is constantly changing. They remind us that sometimes, it is better to blend in than to stand out, to observe quietly and learn from the world around us.

Oh, stick insects, with your slender bodies and delicate limbs, you are the poets of the forest, whispering secrets in the wind. Your presence is a reminder of the interconnectedness of all living things, of the delicate balance that exists in the natural world. You are a symbol of harmony and unity, a testament to the beauty and diversity of life on Earth.

As we watch the stick insects sway and sway in the breeze, we are reminded of our own place in the grand tapestry of existence. We are but one small part of a vast and intricate web of life, connected to all living things in ways we may never fully understand. The stick insects teach us to be humble, to respect and cherish the world around us, for it is a fragile and precious gift that must be protected at all costs.

So let us raise our voices in praise of the stick insects, those silent poets of the forest, and let their beauty and grace inspire us to be better stewards of the Earth. Let us honour their presence in our lives and strive to live in harmony with all living things, for in the end, we are all interconnected, all part of the same great cycle of life.

Haiku about Bearded Dragon

In the desert sun
Bearded dragon basks, content
Golden scales shimmer

Curious eyes watch
Tiny feet explore the world
Silent hunter waits

Underneath the rock
The bearded dragon finds shelter
Ancient guardian

Warm breath on my hand
Bearded dragon whispers
Connection shared

Majestic creature
Bearded dragon, wise and old
Nature's beauty is shown

As we delve deeper into the world of the bearded dragon,
we discover its role as an ancient guardian of the desert.
Seeking shelter beneath the rocks, it stands as a symbol
of resilience and endurance, surviving in harsh conditions
with quiet determination. Through haiku, we pay homage
to this majestic creature, honouring its place in the wild
and celebrating its beauty for all to see.

In the gentle touch of a bearded dragon's breath, we find a connection that transcends words. This silent communication between human and animal speaks volumes about the power of nature to inspire and uplift our spirits. As we read these haiku about the bearded dragon, we are reminded of our shared bond with all living beings, and the beauty that surrounds us in the natural world.

Haiku about Millipede

Haiku, a traditional form of Japanese poetry, is the perfect medium to capture the essence of the millipede, a fascinating creature found in the wild. With its numerous legs and slow, deliberate movements, the millipede is a creature that inspires awe and wonder in those who observe it.

Millipede crawls slow
Legs like delicate branches
Nature's tiny tree

In the forest shade
Millipede moves with grace
Silent symphony

A thousand legs move
In perfect harmony dance
Nature's gentle waltz

Millipede's journey
Through the leaf litter, it roams
Secrets of the Earth

In the twilight hour
Millipede emerges bright
Nature's hidden gem

These haikus capture the essence of the millipede, a creature that often goes unnoticed in the wild but possesses a beauty and grace all its own. Through the simplicity and elegance of haiku poetry, we are able to appreciate the intricate details of the millipede and the important role it plays in the ecosystem. For poetry readers who have a love for animal poetry, these haikus offer a glimpse into the world of the millipede and the wonders of the natural world.

Catfish

In the depths of murky waters, where shadows dance and light barely reaches, swims the mysterious and elusive catfish. With whiskers like delicate threads, they navigate through their underwater world, unseen and silent. Their sleek bodies glide effortlessly, leaving ripples in their wake, a ghostly presence beneath the surface.

In the stillness of the night, when the moon hangs low and the world is hushed in slumber, the catfish emerges from their hiding places. They are the guardians of the river, the silent sentinels of the deep. With eyes that gleam like polished stones, they watch over their domain with a quiet intensity, their ancient wisdom flowing through the currents.

Salmon Leaping

In the heart of the wilderness, where the rivers flow free,
The salmon leap with grace and agility,
Their silvery scales shining in the sunlight,
As they journey upstream with all their might.

The water roars and churns as they make their way,
Up the rapids, through the rocks, they do not sway,
Their instinct drives them on, a force unseen,
To fulfil their destiny, to spawn and preen.

Oh, the beauty of the salmon leaping high,
A sight to behold under the vast sky,
Their bodies glistening in the morning dew,
A testament to nature's wonders, so true.

So let us marvel at these creatures of the stream,
Their determination, their strength, a poet's dream,
For in their journey, we can see our own,
A reminder that we are not alone.

Haiku about Salmon

In the rushing stream
Silver scales flash in the sun
Salmon leap upstream

Through the crystal depths
Majestic salmon swim on
Graceful and serene

In the quiet pool
Salmon rest and wait their turn
To journey upstream

Life cycle complete
Salmon spawn and then they die
Nature's endless loop

In the wild rive
Salmon dance their final dance
A sight to behold

For the poetry readers who appreciate the beauty of
nature and the intricacies of animal life, these haiku
capture the essence of the salmon's journey. From their
graceful movements in the stream to their ultimate
sacrifice for the continuation of their species, these
poems offer a glimpse into the world of these majestic
creatures. Whether you are a lover of animals or simply
enjoy the art of poetry, these haiku about salmon are
sure to resonate with you. Dive into the world of wildlife
poetry and let these verses transport you to the wild
rivers where salmon roam.

Rhino's Charge

In the heart of the savannah, where the sun sets ablaze,
The mighty rhino prowls, its presence a haze.
With skin like armour, and a horn sharp as a spear,
It commands respect, instilling both awe and fear.

When the rhino charges, earth trembles beneath its feet,
A force of nature, unstoppable and complete.
Its eyes ablaze with determination and might,
A sight to behold, a true warrior in the fight.

Through thickets and plains, it charges with grace,
A symbol of strength, a guardian of its space.
In the wild, where danger lurks at every turn,
The rhino's charge reminds us to stand firm.

So let us honour this magnificent beast,
In all its glory, let our admiration never cease.
For in its charge, we find courage and might,
A true testament to the wild's untamed flight.

The Powerful Tiger

In the depths of the dense jungle, a fearsome creature prowls with grace and might. The powerful tiger, with its stripes of gold and black, commands respect and awe from all who dare to cross its path. In this poem, we delve into the essence of this majestic beast, exploring its strength, beauty, and untamed spirit.

The tiger stalks through the shadows, its eyes gleaming with a fierce intensity. With every step, it exudes a primal energy that cannot be tamed or contained. Its muscles ripple beneath its sleek fur, a testament to its raw power and agility. In the silence of the jungle, the tiger moves like a ghost, a silent hunter on the prowl.

As it prowls through the undergrowth, the tiger leaves a trail of fear and awe in its wake. Its roar echoes through the trees, a thunderous sound that strikes fear into the hearts of all who hear it. Yet, despite its fearsome reputation, the tiger is also a creature of beauty and grace. Its coat shimmers in the sunlight, a symphony of colours that blend seamlessly with the jungle around it.

But beneath its beauty lies a fierce and untamed spirit, a reminder of the wildness that lies at the heart of all creatures. The tiger is a symbol of power and strength, a force of nature that cannot be controlled or subdued. In this poem, we pay homage to the mighty tiger, a creature of mystery and wonder that continues to captivate our imagination.

So let us raise our voices in praise of the powerful tiger, a creature of legend and lore that roams the wilds with a grace and majesty that is unmatched. May its spirit inspire us to embrace our own wildness and embrace the untamed beauty of the world around us. In the heart of the jungle, the tiger reigns supreme, a symbol of power and grace that will forever captivate our hearts and minds.

The Magnificent Snow Leopard

In the heart of the snowy Himalayas,
Stalks a creature of mystical grace,
The elusive snow leopard, with its silver coat,
A ghostly presence, a silent remote.

Its magnificent beauty, a sight to behold,
In the rugged mountains, fierce and bold,
Adorned with spots, like stars in the night,
A creature of shadows, a master of flight.

In the depths of winter, it prowls the land,
A silent hunter, with eyes that command,
The frozen landscape, where only the brave tread,
The snow leopard roams, the king of the dead.

Its powerful paws, designed for the snow,
A master of stealth, with nowhere to go,
In the land of ice, it reigns supreme,
The magnificent snow leopard, a creature of dream.

So let us admire this majestic beast,
In the wild, where it roams free and unleashed,
A symbol of beauty, of strength and of grace,
The snow leopard, a creature of wild embrace.

Sleek Leopard

In the heart of the jungle, where the wild things roam,
There lurks a creature never too far from its home,
The sleek leopard, with eyes that gleam,
Moves through the shadows like a silent dream.

Its coat of gold and black, so perfectly designed,
Reflects the beauty of nature, so refined.
In the moonlight, it prowls with grace,
A symbol of power and untamed space.

Its muscles ripple beneath its fur,
As it stalks its prey with a deadly allure.
But in its eyes, there's a hint of sorrow,
A reminder that even the fierce can feel tomorrow.

So let us admire this majestic beast,
In all its glory, at nature's feast.
For in the jungle, where life is wild and free,
The sleek leopard reigns, for all to see.

Gibraltar Monkeys

In the heart of Gibraltar, where the rock meets the sky,
There dwell the monkeys, wild and free, catching the passerby's eye.
Their mischievous antics, their playful ways,
Inspire poets and artists, filling them with praise.

With tails held high and eyes so bright,
These creatures bring joy and awe to all in sight.
Their fur, a mix of brown and grey,
Their presence a reminder of the wild, untamed way.

In poems and songs, their stories are told,
Of ancient legends and tales of old.
They swing from branch to branch, their laughter ringing clear,
In the jungles of Gibraltar, they have nothing to fear.

So let us raise our voices high,
In praise of the Gibraltar monkeys, who soar through the sky.
Their spirit untamed, their hearts so wild,
In the world of poetry, they are forever styled.

The Agile Monkey

In the heart of the jungle, swinging from tree to tree,
There lives a creature that's wild and free.
The agile monkey, with a mischievous grin,
Leaping and bounding with a playful spin.

With limbs so nimble and eyes so bright,
The agile monkey is a captivating sight.
In the canopy, where the sunlight filters through,
He dances and prances, with a joyful hue.

His fur is a tapestry of shades of brown,
Blending in seamlessly with the jungle's crown.
But his spirit is bold, and his energy untamed,
In the wild, he is forever unchained.

So if you ever find yourself in the jungle's embrace,
Listen for the sound of the agile monkey's grace.
For in his movements, there lies a lesson so true,
To live in the moment, and embrace life anew.

The Elegant Jaguar

In the heart of the jungle, where the leaves whisper secrets and the shadows dance with mystery, there prowls a creature of unmatched beauty and grace. The elegant jaguar, with its sleek coat of golden fur adorned with dark rosettes, moves through the dense foliage like a phantom of the night. Its emerald eyes gleam with intelligence and power, a silent predator in a world of chaos.

In the stillness of the moonlit night, the jaguar's presence is felt before it is seen. Its lithe body moves with a fluidity that defies gravity, each step a testament to its strength and agility. The jungle holds its breath as the jaguar stalks its prey, a symphony of life and death playing out in the shadows.

In the silence of the jungle, the jaguar's roar pierces the night like a thunderclap. It is a sound that reverberates through the trees, a primal call that echoes through the ages. The jaguar is a creature of power and majesty, a symbol of the untamed wilderness that lies at the heart of the jungle.

The Graceful Gazelle

In the heart of the jungle, where the trees stand tall and the sun filters through the leaves, there roams a creature so elegant and swift - the graceful gazelle. With delicate hooves that barely make a sound, she moves through the grasslands with a sense of grace that mesmerizes all who are lucky enough to witness her in motion.

Her slender frame is adorned with a coat of earthy tones, blending seamlessly with the golden savannah that is her home. Her eyes, large and doe-like, hold a wisdom that seems to transcend time itself. As she leaps and bounds across the open plains, she embodies the spirit of freedom and wild beauty that is so intrinsic to the jungle.

In the silence of the night, when the stars twinkle above and the moon casts a silver glow over the land, the graceful gazelle dances under the watchful eye of the heavens. Her movements are a symphony of fluidity and poise, a testament to the harmony of nature and the untamed spirit that resides within her soul.

Bison, The Gentle Giant

In the vast expanse of the wild plains,
The bison roams with majestic grace.
Its powerful hooves pound the earth,
A symbol of strength and untamed beauty.

In the stillness of dawn, a bison stands,
Silhouetted against the rising sun.
A creature of ancient wisdom and might,
A guardian of the untamed lands.

Hooves thundering on the open range,
A bison moves with a purposeful stride.
A creature of the prairie, wild and free,
A symbol of resilience and pride.

In the heart of the wilderness, the bison roams,
A creature of the earth, untamed and wild.
Its spirit strong, its presence commanding,
A symbol of nature's power and grace.

In the shadows of the forest, a bison grazes,
A gentle giant in the midst of the trees.
Its soul connected to the ancient rhythms,
A creature of the jungle, wild and free.

The Sleek Weasel

In the undergrowth, the weasel prowls,
Silent and swift, with deadly growls,
Its eyes gleam with a predator's grace,
A creature of the wild, in its rightful place,

With a sleek coat of fur, so dark and sly,
The weasel moves with a cunning eye,
Its whiskers twitch, sensing danger near,
A master of survival, free from fear,

Through the tangled vines, it slinks and creeps,
A shadowy figure, while other creatures are asleep,
In the moon's soft glow, it hunts its prey,
A dance of death, in the light of day,

Oh, weasel of the wild, so fierce and bold,
Your secrets remain untold,
In the heart of the jungle, you reign supreme,
A creature of mystery, a wild, untamed dream.

Haiku about Scorpions

In shadows they hide
Stingers poised and ready to strike
Silent hunter's prowl

Armor of darkness
Creeping through the night unseen
Scorpions thrive alone

Venomous whispers
Nature's fierce protectors lurk
Beneath desert sun

Ancient warriors
Surviving harsh lands with grace
Scorpions endure

Mysterious charm
Intriguing creatures of night
Scorpions enchant us all

These haikus capture the essence of the enigmatic scorpion, a creature both feared and revered in the wild. Their stealthy movements and deadly stingers make them formidable hunters, yet their resilience and adaptability in harsh environments are truly awe-inspiring. From the deserts to the jungles, scorpions are a symbol of survival and strength, embodying the wild spirit of the animal kingdom. Explore the world of scorpions through these poetic verses and discover the beauty and mystery of these fascinating creatures.

Osprey Glide

In the skies, the osprey soar,
Diving swiftly into the river below,
With talons outstretched, it catches its prey,
A magnificent hunter, graceful and bold,

Its wings spread wide, a sight to behold,
Gliding effortlessly through the sky,
A symbol of freedom, of strength, of grace,
The osprey is a creature that will never die,

In the stillness of dawn, its cry can be heard,
Echoing through the trees, a haunting sound,
A reminder of the power of nature,
Of the cycle of life that goes round and round.

Haiku about Locusts

In the jungle's hum
Locust's sing their ancient song
Nature's symphony

Wings shimmering gold
Cascading through the green leave
Locust's dance with grace

Ravenous insects
Feasting on fields of plenty
Harbingers of change

Their numbers multiply
A plague upon the land
Locust's bring both life and death

In their buzzing swarm
Locust's remind us of the
Fragile balance of life

Haiku about Crickets

In the still of night
Crickets' sing their sweet lullaby
Nature's symphony

Tiny musicians
Chirping in the moonlit dark
Their song fills the air

Beneath the jungle canopy
Crickets' serenade the night
Their melody pure

A chorus of chirps
Echoing through the wilderness
Crickets' sing their song

Listen closely now
To the crickets' soothing hum
peaceful and calming

Haiku about Catfish

Slippery whiskers
Hiding in the murky depths
Catfish stalk their prey

Whiskers like fine threads
Tasting the water for food
Catfish glide with ease

Beneath the lily
Catfish waits patiently
For an unsuspecting meal

Silent shadows move
Catfish dart through the water
Swift hunters of the deep

In the jungle's depths
Catfish reign as silent kings
Masters of disguise

Haiku about the Bobcat

Silent hunter stalks
Golden eyes pierce the night sky
Bobcat on the prowl

Graceful predator
Stealthy and swift in the trees
Nature's perfect cat

Whisker's twitching, ears
Alert for the slightest sound
Bobcat waits patiently

Majestic creature
King of the jungle shadows
Bobcat reigns supreme

In the moonlit glade
Bobcat's beauty shines brightly
A wild poetry

Electric Eels Roam

Electric eels, creatures of shock and awe,
In murky waters, they silently draw,

Their power unseen, until they strike,
A flash of lightning, a sudden spike,

In the depths of the jungle, they silently glide,
Electric eels, with their electric pride,

Their bodies pulsing with energy unseen,
A sight to behold, a creature so keen,

In the rivers they dwell, in the darkness they hide,
Electric eels, a force to abide,

With a flick of their tail, a burst of light,
They illuminate the jungle, a stunning sight,

In the poetry of nature, they find their place,
Electric eels, with their electric grace,

Inspiring words of wonder and awe,
In the wild jungle, they leave us in awe,

So let us marvel at these creatures so rare,
Electric eels, with their electric flair,

A look into the electric eel's habitat and home
In the depths of the waters, they silently roam.

The Sea Slug Glides

In the depths of the ocean, a creature so small,
Sea slug glides gracefully, hardly noticed at all,
With colours so vibrant, like a rainbow in the sea,
A mesmerizing sight for all who happen to see,

Soft and squishy, like a jellyfish in disguise,
Sea slug moves with ease, beneath the azure skies,
Its tiny antennas sway in the gentle ocean breeze,
A delicate dance that brings such peace,

In the coral reef, sea slug finds its home,
A world of wonder where it is free to roam,
Among the anemones and the fish so bright,
Sea slug shines like a star in the dark of night,

Oh, sea slug, with your beauty so rare,
In the depths of the ocean, you glide without a care,
A tiny creature with a spirit so free,
You inspire us all by gliding along the bed of the sea.

Haiku about Millipede

In the dense undergrowth of the jungle, the millipede
crawls gracefully, its multitude of legs moving with
effortless fluidity. A creature of mystery and wonder, the
millipede has long fascinated poets and nature lovers
alike. In this subchapter, we explore the beauty of this
remarkable creature through the art of haiku.

Slender legs glide
Through leaves, a silent dancer
Millipede twirls

In the moonlit night
Millipede weaves through shadows
Nature's silent thread

A thousand legs move
In perfect synchrony, a
Living masterpiece

Tiny feet tiptoe
Across the forest floor, a
Whisper in the wind

Millipede's journey
A graceful dance through the wild
Nature's gentle muse

Through these haiku, we glimpse the intricate beauty of the millipede as it navigates its way through the jungle, a silent and graceful presence in the vibrant tapestry of the natural world. Join us on this poetic journey as we celebrate the wonder of jungle creatures through the magic of words.

The Stealthy Leopard

In the heart of the jungle, where shadows dance and melodies of nature fill the air, the stealthy leopard prowls with grace and power. With a coat of golden fur that shimmers in the sunlight, this majestic creature moves like a ghost through the dense foliage, blending seamlessly into its surroundings. Its eyes, sharp and keen, gleam with intelligence and a hint of danger.

In the silence of the night, the leopard hunts with deadly precision, stalking its prey with a patience that is both beautiful and terrifying. With every step, it leaves behind a trail of whispers, a symphony of hushed rustlings that betray its presence to those who dare to listen. In the moonlight, the leopard is a shadowy figure, a fleeting glimpse of pure instinct and primal energy.

In the heart of the jungle, the leopard is a creature of mystery. Its movements are a delicate dance of survival and instinct that speaks to the primal nature of all living things. To witness the leopard in its element is to witness the very essence of the wilderness itself, a reminder of the beauty and danger that lurks just beyond the edge of our civilised world.

The Chinchilla

In the vast and untamed wilderness of Peru,

There exists a creature of delicate beauty and grace,

The chinchilla, with its soft fur and bright eyes,

It moves through the shadows with a quiet elegance'

That captures the hearts of all who behold it,

In the stillness of the night, the chinchilla emerges from its burrow,

Its fur shimmering in the moonlight like a cloak of silver,

As it scampers across the forest floor,

Its tiny paws leave traces of wonder and mystery in their wake,

The chinchilla moves with a swift and silent grace,

A ghostly presence in the shadows of the trees.

Woodpecker Drumming on a Tree

In the heart of the forest, there is a sound,
Of a woodpecker drumming on a tree,
A rhythmic beat that echoes all around,
A symphony of nature, wild and free,

The woodpecker's beak is sharp and strong,
As it pecks and hunts for insects to eat,
Its red head bobs up and down in song,
A beautiful sight, so agile and fleet,

In the quiet of dawn, as the sun rises high,
The woodpecker's call pierces the air,
A reminder that in nature, we are just a small fry,
In the vast wilderness, we must tread with care,

So let us admire the woodpecker's grace,
Its determination, its strength, its pace,
A creature of beauty, in its natural space,
A symbol of nature's wild embrace.

African Elephants

In the vast savannas of Africa, there roams a majestic creature, the African elephant. These gentle giants, with their towering tusks and wrinkled skin, have captivated the hearts of many poets throughout history. Their sheer size and power is a testament to the raw beauty of the natural world, inspiring awe, and reverence in all who witness their grace.

These magnificent beings, with their complex social structures and deep familial bonds, have long been a source of inspiration for poets seeking to capture the essence of the wild.

The African elephant population has been steadily declining due to poaching and habitat loss, making it all the more crucial to raise awareness about the plight of these vulnerable animals.

Black Widow Spider

In the shadows of the night, the black widow spins her web,
A silent predator, waiting for her prey to ebb.
Her sleek black body glistens in the pale moonlight,
A deadly beauty, a symbol of nature's might.

With venomous fangs and a hunger for blood,
She weaves her trap with skill and dexterity, a deadly flood.
Her eight legs move with grace and precision,
A dance of death, a macabre vision.

In the garden, she lurks, a silent killer,
A symbol of fear, a deadly thriller.
But in her dark eyes, there lies a mystery,
A creature of beauty, a symbol of history.

So let us pause and marvel at this creature of the night,
A creature of darkness, a deadly delight.
For in her silent dance, we see the beauty of nature's wrath,
A black widow spider, a symbol of the wild's path.

Haiku about the Huntsman Spider

In the dark forest
Silent spinner waits for prey
Huntsman of the night

Eight legs poised to strike
Silken web a deadly trap
The Skilled predator

Patiently she weaves
Her intricate masterpiece
Nature's architect

Invisible threads
Capture unsuspecting flies
Dinner is served

Weaving in the night
Spider hunts with deadly grace
Nature's silent killer

Haiku about the Picasso Bug

In the wild, hidden,
Picasso bug's vibrant hues
A masterpiece seen

Black and orange stripes
Like a painting on its back
Nature's artistry

Tiny insect, bold
Standing out in the green world
A work of pure art

Picasso bug, small
Yet leaves a big impression
Nature's brush at work

Haiku about Crawfish

In the shallow stream
Crawfish scuttle on the rocks
Shy, yet so vibrant

Their claws snap and click
A dance of survival in
The murky depths below

Mud-stained armour gleams
A creature of mystery
In the river's flow

Ancient guardians
Of the water's hidden depths
Silent and serene

The Swift, Gracious in Flight

In the vast expanse of the wild, there is a creature that captures the imagination with its swift and graceful flight - the swift. With wings that cut through the air like a knife, this majestic bird is a symbol of freedom and agility.

As the swift takes to the air with a burst of speed, it leaves behind all traces of the earth below. Its sleek body glides effortlessly through the clouds, a master of the skies. With every beat of its wings, the swift dances through the air, a vision of elegance and grace.

In the quiet moments of dawn, the swift emerges from its nest, ready to begin a new day of exploration and adventure. With the first light of morning illuminating its wings, the bird takes flight, a blur of movement against the backdrop of the waking world.

As it soars higher and higher into the sky, the swift becomes a symbol of hope and possibility, a reminder that even in the darkest of times, there is always the promise of a new day.

The swift's flight is a testament to the power of nature, a reminder of the beauty and resilience of the natural world. As it navigates the vast expanse of the sky with precision and skill.

In the swift, we see the embodiment of freedom and grace, a creature that embodies the spirit of the wild and reminds us of the wonders that exist beyond our own limited perspective.

So let us raise our voices in praise of the swift, a creature of beauty and wonder that graces the skies with its presence. Let us celebrate the poetry of its flight, the elegance of its movements, and the grace with which it navigates the world. In the swift, we find inspiration and awe, a reminder of the magic and mystery that exists all around us in the heart of nature.

Haiku about a Lioness and Cubs

In the heart of the African savannah, a lioness roams with her precious cubs by her side. Their bond is unbreakable, their love fierce and untamed. In the world of nature, the lioness is the ultimate protector, ensuring the safety and well-being of her young ones as they venture into the wild.

In the shadows of the acacia trees, the lioness watches over her playful cubs, their golden fur glistening in the sunlight. As they pounce and play, she keeps a watchful eye, ready to defend them from any danger that may come their way. In this harsh and unforgiving land, the lioness is a symbol of strength and resilience, a true queen of the wild.

Amidst the tall grasses and swirling dust, the lioness and her cubs move as one, a harmonious dance of survival and love. Their bond is reflected in the poetry of the wind, whispering tales of courage and devotion. In the silence of the night, the lioness's roar echoes through the darkness, a fierce declaration of her fierce protection over her precious offspring.

In the stillness of dawn, the lioness and her cubs bask in the warmth of the rising sun, their silhouettes etched against the golden horizon. In this moment of peace and serenity, the beauty of their bond is captured in a haiku that speaks to the very essence of their existence:

Golden eyes gleaming
Mother's love fierce and untamed
Lioness and her cubs

In the heart of the savannah, the lioness and her cubs stand as a testament to the power and beauty of the natural world. Their story is one of courage, love, and survival, a timeless tale that will forever be etched in the poetry of the wild.

Haiku about the Python

In the depths of the jungle, the python slithers silently, a creature of both beauty and danger. Its scales glisten in the sunlight, a mesmerizing sight for those lucky enough to catch a glimpse. In my haiku poem about the python, I seek to capture the essence of this majestic creature in just a few short lines.

Coiled and ready to strike
Python in the shadows
Nature's deadly grace

The python moves with a grace that belies its deadly potential. In my haiku, I wanted to convey the sense of power and danger that surrounds this magnificent serpent. Its sleek body and penetrating gaze are a reminder of the wildness that still exists in our world, despite our attempts to tame and control it.

In the silence of the jungle
Python waits, patient
Nature's silent predator

The python is a silent predator, waiting patiently for its next meal to come within striking distance. In my haiku, I wanted to capture the sense of stillness and anticipation that surrounds this creature as it lies in wait for its prey. The python is a reminder of the circle of life in the wild, where every creature must hunt or be hunted in order to survive.

Scale by scale, the python
Sheds its old skin
Nature's eternal cycle

Like all creatures, the python must shed its old skin in order to grow and thrive. In my haiku, I wanted to convey the sense of renewal and transformation that comes with this process. The python's discarded skin is a reminder of the eternal cycle of life and death that plays out in the natural world, a cycle that we are all a part of whether we realize it or not.

In the heart of the jungle
Python reigns supreme
Nature's silent guardian

The Wallaby Leaps

Beneath the moonlit sky, the wallaby leaps with grace,
Silent footsteps on the forest floor, a fleeting embrace.

In the stillness of the night, a whisper in the trees,
A gentle spirit roams free, carried by the breeze.

Eyes that reflect the wisdom of the ancient land,
A heart that beats in rhythm with nature's hand.

In the dawn's first light, the wallaby stands tall,
A symbol of resilience, in a world that's bound to fall.

The Yak Grazes

In the vast expanse of the Himalayan mountains,
The yak stands proud and strong,
Its thick fur protecting from the cold,
A symbol of resilience in nature's song.

Majestic creature of the highlands,
With horns that curve like crescent moons,
Graceful in its movements,
A sight that makes the heart swoon.

In the silence of the snowy peaks,
The yak grazes peacefully,
A harmony with the land,
A connection that is truly free.

Oh, noble yak, with eyes that hold wisdom,
A creature of the wild and free,
In your presence, we find solace,
In your grace, we find beauty.

Haiku about Wild Ponies

Wild ponies roam free
Hooves pounding on earth below
Grace in every step

Majestic creatures
Manes flowing in the wind's dance
Eyes full of wisdom

Golden coats shimmer
In the light of the setting sun
Nature's beauty found

In the wild they thrive
Living in harmony with
Land, sea, sky above

Environments of Wild Animals

In the vast and untamed world of nature, wild animals roam freely in a variety of different environments. From the dense forests to the wide-open savannas, each habitat provides a unique setting for these creatures to thrive.

One of the most enchanting environments for wild animals is the lush and vibrant rainforest. Here, the dense canopy of trees provides shelter and protection for a wide array of species, from colourful birds to elusive big cats.

On the other end of the spectrum, the vast expanse of the Arctic tundra offers a stark and unforgiving landscape for wildlife. Here, polar bears and arctic foxes navigate the icy terrain in search of food and shelter.

The open plains of the savanna provide a sweeping backdrop for some of Africa's most iconic wildlife, from the majestic lions to the graceful giraffes.

In the mysterious depths of the ocean, a whole other world exists for wild animals to explore. From playful dolphins to the majestic whales, the underwater realm is a treasure trove of beauty and wonder.

African Wild Animals

In the vast savannas of Africa, where the sun sets in a blaze of colours, the wild animals roam free, embodying the spirit of the untamed wilderness.

The lion, with its mane of gold and fierce, piercing eyes, is the king of the savanna, ruling over his domain with power and grace. His roar echoes across the plains, a symbol of strength and authority that strikes fear into the hearts of all who hear it. Yet even this mighty predator has a softer side, as he nuzzles his cubs and watches over his pride with a sense of pride and devotion.

The elephant, with its massive frame and gentle eyes, moves through the African landscape with a sense of quiet dignity. These majestic creatures are a symbol of wisdom and grace, their wrinkled skin telling the story of a life lived in harmony with the land. As they wander through the forests and grasslands, their presence is a reminder of the importance of protecting the natural world and all its inhabitants.

The giraffe, with its long neck and graceful movements, towers above the trees, a symbol of elegance and beauty in the African wilderness. With their distinctive patterns and gentle demeanour, these gentle giants inspire awe and wonder in all who behold them. As they graze on the leaves of the acacia trees, their presence is a reminder of the delicate balance of nature and the importance of preserving the habitats of these magnificent creatures.

Wild Animals of Madagascar

In the heart of Madagascar, where the wild animals roam,
Lies a land of wonder, a place to call home.
From the lemurs in the trees to the chameleons on the ground,
Every creature here is a treasure to be found.

The ring-tailed lemurs, with their striped tails held high,
Leap from tree to tree, reaching for the sky.
Their playful antics and curious eyes,
Bring joy to all who see them under the African skies.

The fossa prowls through the night, a predator in disguise,
With sharp teeth and keen eyes, it's not one to despise.
This elusive creature, a mix of cat and mongoose,
Is a symbol of the wild, a reminder of nature's use.

The chameleons blend in with their surroundings so well,
Changing colours to match the leaves, a magical spell.
These creatures of camouflage, masters of disguise,
Remind us of the beauty of nature's endless ties.

So let us cherish these animals, so wild and so free,
For they are the heartbeat of Madagascar, the essence of its glee.
In this land of wonder, where the wild things run,
Let us protect and preserve them, for they are second to none.

Turtles Laying Their Eggs on the Beach

In the quiet of the night, under the watchful gaze of the moon, turtles emerge from the depths of the ocean to lay their eggs on the sandy shores. The rhythmic thump of their flippers against the soft sand creates a mesmerising melody, a dance of life and nature intertwined. As they dig their nests and carefully deposit their precious cargo, a sense of wonder and awe fills the air, a testament to the beauty and resilience of these ancient creatures.

The turtles move with grace and purpose, guided by instinct and the pull of the tides. Their ancient eyes gleam with wisdom and determination as they complete their sacred task, ensuring the continuation of their species for generations to come. As they return to the sea, leaving behind a trail of tiny footprints in the sand, a sense of reverence and gratitude fills the hearts of all who witness this miraculous event.

In the hushed stillness of the predawn hours, the beach is transformed into a sanctuary of life and renewal. Each egg laid is a promise of new beginnings, a symbol of hope and resilience in a world fraught with challenges and uncertainties.

As the first light of dawn breaks over the horizon, casting a golden glow over the beach, the turtles' work is done. They slip back into the embrace of the ocean, disappearing beneath the surface with a sense of quiet satisfaction. And as we stand in awe of their grace and beauty, we are reminded of the delicate balance of life on this planet, and the importance of preserving and protecting the natural world for future generations to come.

So let us take a moment to pause and reflect on the wonder of turtles laying their eggs on the beach, a timeless ritual that speaks to the interconnectedness of all living things. Let us be inspired by their courage and determination, their unwavering commitment to the continuation of their species. Let us pledge to be stewards of the earth, to protect and cherish the precious gifts of nature that surround us, now and always.

Haiku about the Pelican

In the vast expanse of the wild, the pelican soars gracefully, its wings outstretched against the azure sky. This majestic bird, with its distinctive bill and striking plumage, is a symbol of freedom and resilience in the natural world.

Beneath the sun's glow
Pelican glides on the breeze
A dance of grace

In the stillness of dawn
Pelican takes flight
Silent guardian of the sea

In the evening's hush
Pelican rests on the shore
A moment of peace

Haiku about the Toucan

Perched high in the trees
Toucan calls with melodic
song of wilderness

Black and white contrast
Toucan's feathers gleam brightly
Nature's monochrome

Toucan's eyes watch close
Guardians of the rainforest
Wise and ancient soul

Majestic toucan
Symbol of the wild and free
Nature's poetry

Haiku about the Jay

In the quiet of the woodland, a jay takes flight,
Its feathers shimmering in the dappled light,
A flash of blue against the green,
A sight to behold, a creature unseen.

Perched upon a branch, it calls out loud,
A raucous cry that pierces the shroud,
Of silence that envelops the woods,
A sound that echoes through the ancient woods.

In three short lines, a haiku is born,
Capturing the essence of the jay at morn,
Its beauty and grace, its wild song,
In words that are simple, yet so strong.

So let us pause and take a moment to see,
The wonder of nature, the jay's symphony,
In poetry's embrace, we find a way,
To celebrate the wild, in a haiku today.

Haiku about the Jackdaw

In the quiet of the forest, a lone jackdaw perches on a branch, its black feathers shining in the sunlight. This mysterious bird, with its piercing eyes and clever nature, has long captured the imagination of poets and artists alike. In this haiku poem, we explore the beauty and wonder of the jackdaw, a creature that embodies the wild spirit of the natural world.

On a windswept bough
Jackdaw caws in the twilight
Echoes of the wild

The jackdaw's call is haunting and melodic, a symbol of the untamed wilderness that lies just beyond our reach. Its dark plumage and sharp beak speak of a creature that is both fierce and graceful, a reminder of the raw power and beauty of the natural world. In this haiku, we are invited to contemplate the jackdaw's place in the grand tapestry of life, and to marvel at the secrets it holds within its enigmatic gaze.

In the depths of winter
Jackdaw dances on the snow
Whispers of the wild

As the seasons change and the world transforms around us, the jackdaw remains a constant presence, a symbol of resilience and adaptability. In this haiku, we see the bird as it frolics in the snow, a fleeting moment of joy and freedom in a world that is constantly in flux. The jackdaw's dance is a celebration of life and a testament to the enduring power of nature, a reminder that even in the harshest of times, beauty and wonder can still be found.

In the heart of the forest
Jackdaw builds its nest of dreams
Guardian of the wild

The jackdaw is a creature of myth and legend, a guardian of the wild places that lie beyond the reach of man. In this haiku, we see the bird as it tends to its nest, a symbol of protection and care in a world that is often harsh and unforgiving. The jackdaw's nest is a sanctuary, a place of safety and solace in a world that is filled with danger and uncertainty. In the jackdaw, we find a kindred spirit, a creature that embodies the wild wonder of the natural world and the enduring power of the human spirit.

Haiku about the Robin

In the early morning light, a robin perches on a tree branch, its bright red breast catching the sun's rays. This common bird, found in backyards and forests alike, inspires awe and wonder with its simple beauty. In the world of wildlife poetry, the robin has long been a muse for poets seeking to capture the essence of nature in just a few short lines.

Red breast in the sun
Singing sweetly in the trees
Robin, joyous one

The Heron

In the stillness of the marsh,
A heron stands tall and proud,
Silent sentinel of the wetlands,
Graceful beauty in the shroud.

With feathers like silk,
And eyes sharp as a spear,
The heron waits patiently,
For fish to come near.

In the calm of the morning,
The heron takes flight,
Wings outstretched in majesty,
A breathtaking sight.

In the dance of the heron,
We see nature's perfect grace,
A reminder of the wild wonders,
That inhabit this sacred place.

So let us pause and marvel,
At this magnificent bird,
A symbol of freedom and beauty,
In every whispered word.

The Stalk, Silent and Strong

In the depths of the forest, a slender stalk stands tall,
Reaching for the sun's warm rays, it's a sight to enthral.
Silent and strong, it sways with the gentle breeze,
A testament to nature's grace and ease.

In the heart of the meadow, a stalk of gold,
Dancing in the wind, a sight to behold.
Graceful and delicate, it bends without a sound,
In harmony with the world around.

In the garden, a stalk stands proud and true,
Bearing the weight of the morning dew.
A symbol of resilience and strength,
In a world where beauty knows no length.

A stalk of green, a stalk of gold,
A story of nature waiting to be told.
In the wild wonder of the world we see,
The beauty of a stalk, simple yet free.

In the silence of the forest, in the song of the breeze,
In the dance of the stalk, we find our peace.
A haiku poem to celebrate this sight,
In the wild wonder of nature's light.

The Swallow

In the vast sky above, a sleek swallow soars,
Swift wings slicing through the air with grace,
A messenger of spring, a symbol of freedom,
In its flight, a dance of beauty and wonder.

In a haiku poem, we capture the essence of this
magnificent bird,
Three lines to convey its spirit and grace,
A fleeting glimpse of nature's perfection,
In the form of seventeen syllables.

A swallow's song, a melody of joy,
Echoing through the meadows and fields,
A chorus of life, a celebration of flight,
In every flutter of its wings.

Oh, graceful swallow, with your iridescent feathers,
A jewel in the sky, a symbol of hope,
In your delicate form, we find solace,
In your flight, we find inspiration.

So let us pause, dear poetry readers,
And pay homage to this wondrous creature,
In the form of a haiku, a small tribute,
To the beauty of the swallow in flight.

Haiku about the Wood Pigeon

Perched on a branch high
Wood pigeon coos its sweet song
Echoes through the trees

Feathers soft as silk
Whispering secrets of flight
In the dappled light

In the quiet woods
Wood pigeon dances on air
Lost in reverie

Majestic and proud
Wood pigeon surveys its realm
King of the treetops

Oh wood pigeon, sing
Your melody fills the air
A gift to us all

Through these haiku poems, we are reminded of the delicate balance of nature and the importance of taking the time to appreciate the beauty that surrounds us. The wood pigeon may be a common sight in the woods, but through the art of poetry, we are able to see it in a new light, as a symbol of grace and harmony in the wild. So let us pause, listen to its song, and marvel at the wonders of the natural world.

Albatross

In the vast expanse of the open sea, the albatross soars gracefully, a symbol of freedom and strength. Its wings span wide, catching the wind with ease, as it glides effortlessly above the waves. This majestic bird is a marvel to behold, inspiring awe and wonder in all who witness its flight.

In the stillness of dawn, the albatross takes flight,
Wings outstretched, dancing on the morning light,
A creature of beauty, grace, and might,
In the endless expanse of the open sea's sight.

With eyes that see beyond the horizon's line,
The albatross navigates the vast ocean's brine,
A master of the skies, a creature divine,
In its presence, we are humbled and refined.

Oh, albatross, with your wings so wide,
You glide through the heavens with effortless stride,
A symbol of freedom, a spirit untied,
In your presence, we find peace and pride.

So let us cherish this bird of the sea,
In its beauty and grace, may we always be free,
For the albatross is a wonder to see,
A true masterpiece of wild poetry.

Haiku about the Black Mamba

Slithering through grass
Black Mamba strikes with deadly speed
Nature's silent death

In shadows it hides
Eyes as dark as night itself
Deadly beauty lurks

Venomous fangs bared
Black Mamba strikes without fear
Silent killer waits

Graceful and deadly
Black Mamba glides through the trees
Nature's silent threat

Respect the Black Mamba
For in its lethal beauty
Wild wonder thrives

Glow-Worm Shines Bright

In the darkness of night, a tiny glow appears,
A glow-worm shines bright, dispelling all fears.
With its luminescent light, it dances and sways,
A mystical creature, in the moon's gentle gaze.
A Haiku poem for this marvel of nature,
A tribute to the glow worm's radiant feature.

In the damp forest floor, the glow-worm thrives,
A magical being, in nature's hidden archives.
Its glow attracts mates, in a mesmerizing dance,
A beacon of hope, in the shadows of chance.
Oh, glow worm, you light up the night,
A symbol of beauty, in the darkness so right.

In the stillness of night, the glow-worm glows,
A sight to behold, as the moon softly bestows.
Its light brings wonder, to all who behold,
A creature so small, yet its brilliance untold.
Let us cherish this creature, so rare and unique,
A marvel of nature, so humble and meek.

In the depths of the forest, the glow-worm shines,
A tiny beacon, in the darkness it defines.
Its light guides the lost, through the shadows of fear,
A touch of magic, that is always near.
Oh, glow worm, you light up the night,
A symbol of hope, in the dimmest twilight.

So let us celebrate the glow-worm's glow,
A wonder of nature, in the darkness below.
For in its light, we find peace and delight,
A reminder of beauty, in the stillness of night.
To the glow worm, we raise our voices in praise,
A creature so wondrous, in nature's wild maze.

Haiku about the Dune Bug

In the vast desert sands of the American Southwest, a tiny creature scurries along the dunes, its iridescent shell shimmering in the sunlight.

Beneath the hot sun
Dune Bug scuttles on the sand
A jewel in the dust

With wings like stained glass
Fluttering in the desert breeze
Nature's tiny gem

In the silence of
The desert night, Dune Bug hums
A lullaby song

Among the shifting
Dunes, Dune Bug dances freely
A creature of light

In the harsh desert
Dune Bug thrives, a testament
To nature's wonders

The Oyster Catcher

In the vast expanse of the shore,
Oyster Catcher dances and soars,
Its beak sharp as a dagger,
Searching for treasures by the water.

Black and white feathers gleam,
Against the backdrop of the ocean's dream,
A flash of red around its eyes,
As it hunts for food with skilful guise.

With a haunting cry that pierces the air,
Oyster Catcher announces its presence without a care,
A sentinel of the shoreline, proud and free,
In harmony with the rhythm of the sea.

Oh, magnificent bird of the coast,
Your beauty and grace we cherish most,
In the world of salt and sand,
You are a symbol of nature's grand.

In a haiku, we capture your essence,
Oyster Catcher, bird of opulence,
Majestic hunter of the sea,
Forever wild and untamed, you will be.

Haiku about the Duck Billed Platypus

In murky waters
Duck billed platypus swims by
Nature's oddity

Unique creature of
Australia's rivers and streams
Platypus glides on

Mammal, bird, reptile
A mix of species in one
Platypus amazes

Bill like a duck's, fur
soft as a mammal's, platypus
truly one of a kind

Let us marvel at
Nature's creativity
In the platypus

Haiku about the Dung Beetle

In the world of wildlife, the humble dung beetle often goes unnoticed, tirelessly rolling dung balls across the savannah. In this haiku poem about the dung beetle, we seek to capture the essence of this hardworking creature in just a few short lines

Rolling in the dirt
Dung beetle's noble mission
Nature's janitor

With strength and purpose
Pushing dung through grassy fields
A quiet hero

In the heat of day
Dung beetle toils away
Nature's work unseen

Tiny black beetle
Carrying the weight of worlds
In silence it sings

Oh dung beetle, how
Your humble task inspires us
In your work we find peace

Haiku poem about the Dormouse

Silent as moonlight
Dormouse slips through shadows deep
Nature's hidden gem

In the darkness of night, the dormouse emerges from its
cozy burrow, venturing out to search for food and explore
its surroundings. With keen senses and a cautious
nature, it navigates the forest floor with grace and agility.
As it moves with careful precision, it leaves behind a trail
of wonder and enchantment for those lucky enough to
witness its delicate movements.

Whisker's quiver, eyes bright
Dormouse dances in moonlight
Nature's gentle sprite

The dormouse is a creature of mystery and magic, a
reminder of the untamed beauty that exists in the world
around us. Its presence is a gift, a reminder to slow down
and appreciate the small wonders that surround us each
day. In the quiet moments of solitude, we can find
inspiration and solace in the company of the door mouse,
a symbol of resilience and grace in a world that often
moves too fast.

In the heart of the forest
Dormouse finds solace and peace
Wild wonder revealed

Haiku about Rainbow Trout

In the crystal waters
Rainbow trout dance with the sun
Nature's vibrant art

Their scales shimmer bright
A rainbow beneath the wave
Graceful and serene

In rivers they glide
Majestic creatures of the depths
Symbols of freedom

With each graceful leap
They defy gravity's pull
A fleeting moment

Oh, rainbow trout dear
Your beauty captures our hearts
Wild wonder untamed

Haiku about the Rattlesnake

In the heart of the desert
Rattlesnake coils quietly
Nature's deadly grace

Silent slithering
Venomous fangs poised to strike
A predator's dance

Rattlesnake's warning
Nature's elegant alarm
Respect her power

Camouflaged beauty
Desert's sleek predator
Survival's song sung

In the wild, beware
Rattlesnake's lethal embrace
Nature's silent threat

The Honey Bear

In the dense forest, a honey bear roams,
With golden fur that shines like sunlight's beams.
Stealthy and swift, it moves with grace,
In search of sweet nectar to embrace.

Its playful antics, a joy to behold,
As it dances through the trees so bold.
With a gentle demeanour, yet fierce in its way,
The honey bear brightens up the day.

In the quiet of the night, it rests its head,
Dreaming of the honeycomb it will soon be fed.
A creature of wonder, so wild and free,
The honey bear embodies true beauty.

So let us celebrate this creature rare,
With a haiku poem that captures its flair.
In the heart of the forest, where wild things roam,
The honey bear finds its truest home.

Haiku about the Mosquito

Buzzing in the night
Tiny predator of blood
Nature's nuisance thrives

With silent approach
Needle nose pierces the skin
Leaving behind itch

Summer symphony
Mosquitoes hum in the air
Uninvited guests

Their tiny bodies
Carriers of disease and pain
Nature's cruel jesters

Despite their annoyances, mosquitoes are an integral
part of the ecosystem. They serve as a food source for
many animals and help pollinate flowers.

Haiku about Wasps

In the buzzing world of wildlife, wasps are often seen as a nuisance, but in the world of poetry, they can inspire beauty and wonder.

Golden wings shimmer
Buzzing in the summer heat
Nature's warriors

This simple yet powerful poem captures the energy and beauty of the wasp as it flits through the summer air. The golden wings symbolise the delicate beauty of these creatures, while the buzzing evokes their ever-present energy and vitality.

Haiku about the Crocodile

In the murky waters
A crocodile lies in wait
Silent, patient, still

Sharp teeth gleaming white
Eyes watchful, calculating
Nature's ancient guard

In the river's flow
The crocodile hunts its prey
A sleek, deadly force

Powerful jaws snap
Life ends in an instant
Nature's balance kept

So let us marvel
At the crocodile's fierce grace
In the wild wonder

Haiku about the Gopher

In tunnels deep below
Gopher scurries, hides from sight
Nature's engineer

Tiny paws dig fast
Creating homes underground
Labyrinths of earth

Soft fur, curious eyes
Gopher explores its domain
Nature's busy friend

Silent sentinel
Gopher stands guard in the grass
Watching, waiting, still

In harmony with
The earth, the sky, the seasons
Gopher lives and thrives

For poetry readers who appreciate the beauty of wildlife, the haiku poem about gopher captures the essence of this small, yet remarkable creature. Through vivid imagery and concise language, the poem paints a picture of the gopher's industrious nature as it tunnels through the earth, creating intricate networks of underground homes. The haiku also highlights the gopher's role as a vital part of the ecosystem, serving as a silent sentinel in the grass, always watchful and in tune with the rhythms of nature.

Haiku about the Dingo

In the vast outback of Australia, the dingo roams free, a symbol of untamed wilderness and natural beauty.

Beneath the moon's glow
Dingo's howl fills the night air
Echoes of wildness

In the red desert
Dingo tracks in the sand blend
A ghost of the wild

Swift and silent hunter
Dingo prowls through the brush
Nature's perfect predator

In the golden light
Dingo dances with the wind
A wild spirit free

Haiku about the Grasshopper

Grasshopper leaps high
In a field of emerald green
Chirping a sweet song

This simple yet elegant haiku poem captures the essence of the grasshopper in its natural habitat, showcasing its beauty and grace. The imagery of the emerald green field and the sweet song of the grasshopper evoke a sense of peace and harmony with nature.

Haiku about the Crane

Gentle giant soars
Graceful wings against blue sky
Beauty in motion

Feathers like silk thread
Dancing in the morning light
Cranes in harmony

Majestic crane calls
Echoes through the tranquil marsh
Nature's symphony

Stilted legs in flight
Balancing on fragile reeds
A delicate dance

In ancient folklore
Cranes are symbols of wisdom
Guiding us through life

Haiku about Various Animals and Insects

Minute flapping wings
Ladybird, all red and black
Natural beauty

Butterfly swooping
Then lands on a flower
Soaks up the sun

Deer stand silent
Observing and listening
On a remote glen

Bumblebee's zoom
Yellow and black stripes
Always in a rush

Wasps in their nests
Zoom, buzz, hum, whizz
They fly at such speed

A stag transfixed
Motionless for a time
Then sprints away

Frogs partner-up
Mating time is here
So spawny!

The buzz and humming
As bees hunt for pollen
Whoosh! Now they're gone

Frogs roam in droves
With a chorus of croaks
Covered in slime

Squirrels foraging
Horse chestnuts being buried
Their hidden gems

A prickly hedgehog
Roaming in the grass
Finding slugs and snails

Birds bees and insects
Busy all day feeding
They chirp, buzz and crawl

Birds build their nests
Collecting Straw and twigs
All with their beaks

Birds in the trees
Chirping and whistling
While they peck and feed

Seagulls swarming
Over towns and beaches
In search of food

Birds build their nests
Lay their eggs, incubate
Crack! New life is born

Snails slither along
Their world in slow motion
Trailblazers!

Wild feral cats
Chasing rabbits, their prey
Fast and furiously

Birds awaken
Dancing shuffling feet
Feeding frenzy begins

Birds of prey
Roaming overhead
Patrolling the skies

Turquoise blues and greens
Dragonflies swoop and fly
Iridescent flashes

Bees buzzing around
From flower to flower
Collecting pollen

Woodlice crawl
Over the decaying bark
Of dead fallen trees

Wild deer drift by
Eating grass and plants
Shy and timid

Sheep graze fields
Grassland hills and moors
Munching aimlessly

Spiders web
Covered in morning dew
Glisten and sparkle

The crafty red fox
Stalking chickens and sheep
Always on the prowl

Red robin flitters
As he sings his songs
Zoom! then he's gone

Wings beating fast
Dragonfly in mid-flight
Majestically coloured

A spider waits
Hanging upon its web
For fresh prey

Grasshopper jumps
Springing into action
Boing, Boing!

Dove's so elegant
Pristine white feathers
Peace and harmony

Cockroaches' crawl
Resilient creatures
They get everywhere

Mallard ducks' glide
Along the river waters
Quacking all the way

Horses running wild
In the fields so green
Majestic at play

Woodpigeon coo
In the treetops above
Such free spirits

Magpie swoop down
They'll pinch what they can
Nature's thieves

Crocodiles stealthy
Natural born killers
With no remorse

Shetland ponies
Horses but in miniature
So cute and sweet

Swallows flitter
Swooping and diving
Feeding time

Field mice scurry
Keeping hidden from sight
In amongst the crops

Glow worm
Lighting up the night
Natures glow sticks

Robin's fluttering
Tiny red bellied beauties
Swishing and swooping

Stag beetle
Shimmering in black
With large pincer claws

Majestic in black
Raven' watch intensely
All perched on fences

Dingo's prowl
Hunting for prey
Circling in a pack

Ladybird's, so pretty
But neither a lady nor a bird
It's a bug's life

Heron, tall and proud
With their long necks
Such a stretch

Bird's flying in flocks
Like a dark cloud overhead
Ever changing patterns

Otter leap and bound
In and out of the water
Never still for long

The Wonder of Creation

In the vast expanse of the natural world, there is a beauty that cannot be captured in words alone. It is the wonder of creation, the intricate dance of life that unfolds before our eyes each day. From the majestic mountains to the smallest insects, every creature plays a vital role in the delicate balance of our ecosystem.

As poetry readers, we are drawn to the wild wonder of the world around us. We find solace in the songs of the birds, the rustling of the leaves, and the gentle flow of the rivers. Through the power of language, we seek to capture the essence of these moments, to pay tribute to the creatures that inhabit our planet.

Wildlife poetry allows us to delve into the mysteries of the natural world, to explore the hidden depths of the forests and the secrets of the oceans. Through the eyes of a poet, we can experience the world in a new light, seeing the beauty and complexity of nature with fresh eyes. Each poem is a tribute to the wonders of creation, a celebration of the diversity and resilience of the creatures that share our world.

In the wild wonder of creation, we find inspiration and awe. We are reminded of the interconnectedness of all living things, of the delicate balance that sustains life on Earth. Through poetry, we can share in the joy and wonder of the natural world, and perhaps, in doing so, inspire others to cherish and protect the creatures that call our planet home.

So let us revel in the beauty of the world around us, let us be grateful for the wonders of creation that surround us each day. Through the power of poetry, we can pay tribute to the wild creatures that bring us joy and wonder, and perhaps, in doing so, inspire others to see the world through new eyes.

Threatened Species

In the vast and diverse world of wildlife, there are countless species that are currently facing the threat of extinction. These threatened species are in danger of disappearing forever if we do not take action to protect and preserve them. From majestic big cats like the amur leopard to tiny insects like the rusty patched bumblebee, every creature plays a vital role in the delicate balance of our planet's ecosystems.

As lovers of poetry, we have the unique opportunity to raise awareness and advocate for these endangered creatures through the power of words. By crafting poems that celebrate the beauty and importance of threatened species, we can inspire others to join in the fight to save them from extinction. Through our words, we can shine a spotlight on these often-overlooked animals and remind the world of their value and worth.

In the silence of the forest, the cry of the red wolf echoes through the trees. Once abundant across North America, these elusive predators now teeter on the brink of extinction. Through poetry, we can capture the spirit of the red wolf and convey the urgency of their plight. By weaving together vivid imagery and heartfelt emotions, we can create a lasting tribute to these magnificent creatures and inspire others to take action to protect them.

The pangolin, with its armour-like scales and gentle demeanour, is another species that is facing imminent extinction due to poaching and habitat loss. In our poetry, we can paint a portrait of this unique and endearing creature, highlighting its importance in the ecosystem and the urgent need for conservation efforts to save it from disappearing forever. Through our words, we can evoke empathy and compassion for the pangolin and ignite a sense of responsibility to protect all endangered species.

As wildlife poetry enthusiasts, we have a powerful platform to raise awareness and advocate for threatened species. Through our poems, we can amplify the voices of the voiceless and shine a light on the urgent need for conservation efforts to save these creatures from extinction. Let us harness the beauty and power of poetry to inspire change and protect the precious wildlife that enriches our world.

Printed in Great Britain
by Amazon

40121792R00175